AF798530

THE TOONALUTION OF BIG BUSINESS

Toon-a-lu-tion
[Toon-*ah*-**loo'**-sh*u*n] - *noun*
The evolution from a realistic,
complex form to a
simplistic, cartoon form

written & illustrated by:
Greg Stanley

As a thank you for your support, please visit an author signing event to receive your FREE Toonalution self-portrait with the Toonalution characters!

To Start Your Own Toonalution, go to www.toonalution.com

Toon-a-lu-tion [Toon-*ah*-**loo'**-sh*u*n] - *noun*
The evolution from a realistic, complex form to a simplistic, cartoon form

A special thanks to my wonderful wife and partner, Jenni, for her limitless support, discerning opinions and unflappable patience with my crazy questions such as "If you were an unemployed appendix and in a talent show, what would your talent be?"

Jenni's Toonalution captures her penchant for working on many projects at one time including stamping, crafting and quilting. Love you Sweetie!

"Every morning in Africa, a Gazelle wakes up. It knows it must run faster than the fastest lion or it will be killed.

Every morning in Africa, a Lion wakes up. It knows it must outrun the slowest Gazelle or it will starve to death.

It doesn't matter whether you are a Lion or a Gazelle... when the sun comes up, you'd better be running." - African proverb

Throughout this book, we will follow Jay Gregory, a fictional character who represents the everyday employee as he goes on an adventure through the World of Big Business.

CONTENTS

JAY GREGORY, 23, FRESH OUT OF BUSINESS SCHOOL
EXPERIENCE? LACKING. MOTIVATION? STRONG.
DESIRE TO PROVE HIMSELF? OFF THE CHARTS.
BIG BUS
FUTURE? ONE BIG ADVENTURE
OBSTACLES? TOO MANY TO COUNT.

PREFACE: A MULTITUDE OF MOMENTS

Like many events in life, this book is the culmination of a multitude of moments. I feel fortunate that I have been able to see this to publication because its creation has encompassed all aspects of my life: professional, spiritual and personal. I have been blessed by the people with whom I work, the friends with whom I associate, my family and my wonderful wife, Jenni. Thank you for all of your support.

The first moment is, unfortunately, a tragedy. It is being mentioned because it involves my employer and the circumstances in which my parents first met over fifty years ago.

An explosion claimed four lives at the Anchor Hocking glass plant in Winchester, Indiana. The exposition occurred around 7:20 p.m. on June 28, 1957 and was precipitated by the rupturing of a compressed air line. The on-duty foreman, Sterling Banning, heard the blast and witnessed the smoky-orange glow on the horizon from his farm which was five miles away. Even though he was scheduled to work that afternoon, he had switched shifts to accommodate his wife's doctor's appointment. Now, panicked at the unknown, he left his elder daughter, Sharon, in charge of her younger siblings, Linda and Jack.

In the weeks following the explosion, Sterling could not shake the thought that if he had been there, if he was overseeing his men, they may not have been lost. Within two months of the explosion, Sterling was unable to continue working at the site of the tragedy and he transferred to Jacksonville, Florida. Anchor Hocking had recently secured a contract with Maxwell House Coffee to produce a 15oz glass jar for its decaffeinated coffee line. By the three month anniversary of the tragedy, Sterling and his family were beginning their new life as Floridians, 894 miles away from Winchester, Indiana.

John Gilbert Stanley Sr. had been an employee of Maxwell House Coffee for over six years when he finally got the call. The call was a promotion to Plant Engineer at Maxwell House's newly acquired plant in Jacksonville, Florida. In September of 1953, John moved his family from Brooklyn, New York to Jacksonville in pursuit of a position he had been after for some time. He remained in this position until he retired after 32 years of service. In 1989, Maxwell House Coffee became a part of the Kraft Foods family.

On February 15th of 1959, the daughter of Sterling Banning and the son of John Gilbert Stanley Sr., would meet on a blind date and get married eleven months later. In 1971, this daughter would have a son of her own, me. This is moment number one.

Many employees do not consider their employer as being invested in their long-term growth as an asset to the success of their company. Luckily, I am not one of those individuals. For over twenty years I have worked for Kraft Foods and I have been fortunate to not only have managers who have had my career interests in mind, but to also have a company that provides employees with the resources to "raise the bar" on their own performance expectations. This book is the result of such a challenge given to me in 2003. This is moment number two.

Kraft conducts annual and mid-year MAP, Managing & Appraising Performance, review sessions that quantifies an employee's performance against set goals, identifies new performance goals and helps an employee develop their skill sets for their desired career path. This process is well respected internally at Kraft and their efforts to build a better sales force was recognized in 2009 by Cannondale's Annual Power Ranking as the #1 sales force nationally.

My MAP challenge, given to me in 2003 by my then manager, Bruce Cox, was to improve my presentation skills by joining a public speaking club. I would be judged on how effectively I integrated new speaking skills such as the use of humor, eye contact or hand gestures into ten increasingly more complex speeches before I would reach the first level of speaker certification.

At the time, I was managing and coaching a team of fourteen sales representatives and twenty-five full and part-time merchandisers. During my tenure as their manager, I noticed many of them did not grasp some of the basic fundamentals of business. This lack of understanding ranged from how to prepare for an interview to how to market themselves in pursuit of a desired position. Their lack of understanding led to feelings of frustration and discontent that, rightly or wrongly so, were directed at the company for which they worked. These are the people for whom this book is written, whether they are a new college graduate with two weeks experience or a twenty-year vet who wishes to progress to the next level of responsibility.

For the speaking club, it did not matter what subject I spoke about, so I wrote speeches on how "big business" worked. I presented them in creative and fun ways that were accessible to anyone, no matter their level of business experience.

The first three speeches were met with great success. The lessons were learned and everyone enjoyed my creative take on business by using everyday objects and situations. It was suggested by one of my colleagues that I expand the ten speeches and compile them into a book that would be accessible to more people. This book is the result of that suggestion.

The path to publishing was long and fraught with many dead ends and false starts. It's taken over seven years from my MAP review to completion. During my initial foray into publishing, I collected many, many rejection letters from publishers and agents. As a way to garner support for the book, I auctioned off "characters" to real people for each chapter on eBay. On top of all this, I decided to pen over two-hundred illustrations myself.

Over the timeframe it took me to write this book, I have finished my Business Management degree, married, was promoted four times, downsized once, moved three times and logged over 400,000 miles on a multitude of company cars. Life has a way of happening when you're not looking.

Throughout all of this, I have been fortunate to have an employer such as Kraft Foods. Kraft provides resources such as a Leadership Competency Model to identify the paths to upper level positions, the MAP process to provide transparency to management on employees' performance and tuition reimbursement for continuing learning. Kraft provides the resources for all employees to succeed, but it is up to the employee to take the first step on their career path.

My own career path reflects this. I didn't join Kraft as a college graduate fresh out of business school with my MBA. I did it the hard way. I did it the "leave college before finishing without a clue as to what I want to do" way and managed to find a great career.

I began what would eventually be my career with Nabisco, prior to Kraft's acquisition in 2001, as a part-time summer representative stocking cookies and crackers. This wasn't my dream job but it did help pay for college tuition. I quit college after four years of what most people would call a lack of focus, but what I called "conflicting interests." These interests ranged from music to art to architecture to computer science to writing. I went to college on a music scholarship, switched to computer science and thought I found my career calling with architecture. But, by the time most students were graduating, I was looking for a change of scenery from both an educational and geographical point-of-view. I moved to Atlanta after securing a full-time merchandising position with Nabisco making less than $8.00 an hour. My Kraft career began silently, without much fanfare, direction or drive.

But as someone who has a high standard of performance, I continued to receive minor promotions as Nabisco went through reorganizations and the acquisition by Kraft Foods. Eventually, I was given an opportunity to sink or swim on a high profile territory as a Sales Representative. Still unsure of what I wanted to be when I grew up, I pursued a degree in Art Direction from Atlanta's Creative Circus as an outlet for my creative side.

In 2001, I was promoted to an entry level management position responsible for the training and leading of a small team of merchandisers. I enjoyed the experience so much that I put all other pursuits on hold and gave my full effort towards building the best team I could. This was the point, eleven years into my "career" that I thought I would "officially" pursue a career at Kraft Foods. This is moment number three.

As a way to do this, I took advantage of Kraft's Leadership Competency Model to map out my career path. I utilized our MAP process and identified developmental opportunities and communicated my career desires to upper management. I went back to college through the tuition reimbursement program and received my business management degree. Shortly after completing my degree, I was promoted to Retail Sales Manager responsible for thirty-nine full and part-time employees. This would be the best, and the hardest, job I had ever experienced.

As I progressed to other positions on my career path, I had the unfortunate experience of having my position downsized. My wife and I moved to Florida for a position that would provide the experience needed for me to continue on my career path. This learning role became expendable as cost-cutting measures came into effect. Even though I had nineteen years with Kraft at this point, I was the least senior member on the team and the last to join. This was not a great combination for job security. Thankfully, my network of coworkers, managers and my previous management and retail experience allowed me to secure a position in another division.

Christianity is new to me. I'm several years into the believer burn and I still have more questions than answers. But that's not the point. The walk of faith is. I've learned much in my short time: I've learned that I need a weekly worship service to keep my burden bearable; I've learned that being patient means to suffer in silence, and I've learned that the one thing all Christians have in common is that we all fail daily and cannot survive without divine intervention. I've also learned that my desire to be creative, to express myself in a way that helps others, should not be ignored. This is moment number four.

Writing a book is not easy. It is a long and laborious task that seems to have no end. Thankfully, I saw a sign that put the effort of writing a book into a more manageable perspective. It was literally, a sign. It was one of those large, yellow "SHARP TURN COMING" signs with the three-foot, eight-inch black arrows that are prevalent on the switchback roads in north Georgia where crazy crotch rocket fanatics and even crazier cyclists spend their Saturday mornings playing chicken with the locals in their rust covered pickups and the fleeing suburbanites in their kayak crowned SUVs.

I observed one of these signs while I waited with my friend for an ambulance after he high-sided his motorcycle on his first run through Hwy 129 headed north from the one stop-signed town of Suches. It took a smattering of touch up paint to fix the bike; it took a nine inch bolt to fix my friend's shoulder. GA Hwy 129: 1 Buddy: 0. As I contemplated the dynamics of "UH-OH" physics, I became fixated on that sign verses the paint-faded "Black Trout Farm" one next to it. I guess it was because one was more "common" than the other.

Have you ever thought about the effort behind such a word as the word "Common"? Common implies many things. The first is that an item is easy to find or an event occurs on a regular basis. The second, less obvious implication is that this commonality was born out of either extreme need or extreme success. An example of extreme success would be the average cockroach. Sixteen million years old and counting. Able to adapt to many extreme environments, the roach will be here for many more millions of years eating our food, living in our walls and scaring our spouses.

An example of extreme need would be transportation safety. Imagine the number of lives lost or severely impacted by the absence of street signs during the brief history of the internal combustion engine. I do not know how many accidents must occur before a government body decides to invest in new street signs, but I imagine it is costly from both an emotional and financial point of view.

I stood there contemplating the effort it took over time to place that yellow "SHARP TURN COMING" sign with the three-foot, eight-inch black arrows on highway 129 six miles north of Suches right past Black Trout fish pond. I thought back to the inception of this process many, many years earlier, before the sign was made, with the invention of metallurgy processing. Then I worked through the development of the transportation infrastructure in America, the evolution of the automobile, the expansion of settlers into north Georgia following the gold rush of 1848, the governmental bureaucracy of the Department of Transportation, the budget constraints of the local government and the many traffic accidents that must have occurred on this curve to warrant such a sign as warning to coming motorists. This was a great effort that involved an investment in time, resources and life into its placement on that corner of Hwy 129 in the north Georgia Mountains.

I realized that compared to the effort it took to place the yellow "SHARP TURN COMING" sign with the three-foot, eight-inch black arrows on a sharp turn on Highway 129 six miles north of Suches right past Black Trout Fish pond, writing a book would be easy. I just hope my friend sees my book. This is the last moment, moment number five.

I could not have completed this book without the support of the auction winners. As I mentioned, I auctioned off eleven real life "characters" on eBay as a way to generate excitement for the book and it was a great experience on many levels.

First, it brought together a large group of total strangers who have nothing in common other than interest in my creative efforts. Second, it was an auction to be a character in a book which, as far as I know, has never been done before. Third, it transitioned my writing experience from a single person effort into a group effort. Fourth, and most importantly, it compiled a group of diverse people with an incredible array of experience, skills and talents.

At the time of the auction, winners' ages ranged from 21 – 90 years old, education ranged from high school diploma to doctorate degree, career stages from first job to retirement after a 42 year career, geography spanned coast to coast, included union and non-union employees, blue collar and white collar workers, private companies, public companies, Fortune 500 organizations and small businesses. The auction experience broadened my initial audience making it more inclusive, diverse and applicable to more people across the country. Thank you to all of the winners for your support.

This multitude of moments culminated into a desire to do something of significance that would impact other people in a positive way. All that was needed was a catalyst to take action. My MAP review in 2003, where I was challenged to improve my professional skill sets, was that catalyst. I hope you find your catalyst that will inspire you to do something extraordinary that affects others in positive ways. It may come from the ashes of a catastrophe, from an initiative at work, from your house of worship, or, from something as common as a street sign. Wherever it comes from, own it to its completion.

TOONALUTION #1 - Understanding Your place in the Big Picture

John Stanley uses the dinner tray as leverage in a vain attempt to achieve some level of comfort. A fourteen hour overseas flight, even in first class, has a way of working negatively on a person's body. Having celebrated his seventieth birthday this year, John is beginning to feel his age since leaving Atlanta's Hartsfield International Airport nine hours ago. He wonders how difficult it will be to adjust to the time zone difference once they arrive in Tokyo. While he is looking forward to landing and stretching his tired arms, legs and back, he is not looking forward to the three hour train ride they will have to take to reach Misowa, Japan in two days where his elder daughter, Jennifer, lives with her husband, Aaron, and their four-year old daughter, Samantha.

Once he has repositioned himself, John scans the airline magazine that has been hopelessly dog-eared by passengers on previous flights. After flipping through many pages of advertisements and "Ten Best" lists of exotic travel destinations, an article catches his attention. It reviews the 2004 theft of the Edvard Munch paintings The Scream and the Madonna from the Munch Museum in Oslo, Norway. After two years of investigations, both paintings were eventually recovered in the fall of 2006. Emotional and vibrant, The Scream painting helped Munch become a major influence in the beginnings of the 20th Century Expressionist movement.

John's attention fixates on the facial expression on the agonized figure that was the subject of the painting. John is thankful that he is not experiencing any fear or anxiety presently, especially since he is currently flying 37,000 feet over the Pacific Ocean.

The magazine article about travel destinations reminds him of a promise he and his wife of fifty-one years, Sharon, set years ago. From the time they first got married, they made it a point to have travel, and the teachings that come with travel, to be a big part of their family's lives. Having visited forty-nine of the fifty states and 20 countries, they did not let having three children slow them down. Now retired, they live near Atlanta, Georgia, and have found that they are busier in their retirement lives than they were in their professional lives. Most of their travel time is spent visiting those children, Jennifer, Greg and Tara, who live in Japan, Ohio and Washington State respectively. They plan on finishing their tour of the fifty-states with a vacation in Hawaii very soon.

As John puts the magazine back, he closes the airline window shade to attempt to take a nap. He reflects on his years as an educator and as a nurse. He realizes that his level of success was not without many struggles, some of them he won, others he did not.

One challenge that he overcame early on was his ability to understand how his position fit into the organization that employed him. Whether it was as a teacher at a high school, an administrator at a college or as a nurse at a hospital, he found that the better he understood his place within the organization's "big picture," the easier it was for him to succeed. He was sure of one thing, at no time during his career was he as lost in the "big picture" as the poor fellow in the Scream painting.

Dr. John Stanley has never been one to shy away from bettering himself. Not satisfied with a double major in psychology and history and a distinguished career as an educator, he pursed a path of continual learning by earning three more college degrees. He received his Master of Arts in Teaching from Jacksonville University and a Doctor of Philosophy with major in Higher Education from Florida State University in 1980. John's last degree was completed after he retired from the education field. He received his Associate in Science for Nursing from the University of the State of New York at the age of 53 which began his second career as a registered nurse.

John's first "career" job after graduating from college was teaching sixth graders science for one semester at Reynolds Lane Elementary School in Jacksonville, Florida which led to a full time position for three years at Paxon Junior High School. While there, he became the head of the Science Department and revamped the existing program with new initiatives such as conducting lab sessions to keep students excited about school.

John's longest teaching career occurred when he joined Florida Community College at Jacksonville (FCCJ), which was then named Florida Junior College, as a Social Studies professor. This is where John's understanding of how he fit into the "big picture" really came into its own. Because of this understanding when he became department chairman, he was able to excel at managing his employees as well as meeting the expectation of his managers.

During his twenty-five year tenure at FCCJ, John occupied the positions of the Director of Evening Studies, the Division Chairman of the Fine Arts and Language department, led an Off Campus program initiative and the implementation of the Program Afloat College Education (PACE).

John's view of the big picture at FCCJ included understanding his position as a mediator between his faculty and upper management. As in most companies, departments within colleges often pursue what is in their best interest and have blinders on to what might be best for the organization as a whole. John often found himself balancing budget cuts from upper management with financial requests from faculty initiatives. While he got along well with everyone, he sometimes had to reject requests because they were either not financially feasible or not congruent with the goals of the college.

Sometimes, John was able to keep both parties happy by addressing the budget concerns by sourcing revenue thru development of non-credited courses. These courses were created as a way to address needs within the local community. Courses ranged from administrative classes such as typing to language classes to community service opportunities. Each class added financial resources that could be accessed for other causes. Over his tenure, John was able to secure significant assets such as a grand piano for the music department, an art gallery for the south campus and departmental scholarships.

After his career as a professor, John taught gifted and advance placement student

American History and Social Studies for five years at Sandlewood High School and officially retired as an educator in 2004.

When John went back to school to get his nursing degree, he went to fulfill his desire to help others through the medical field. He worked in many diverse environments as a nurse for nine years. He worked for the Department of Corrections at Union Correctional Institution in Raiford, FL. He worked for Columbus, GA HCA Behavior Medicine and for Vista Care Hospice where he traveled from Texas to New England verifying procedural compliance. John retired for a second time in 2006 as a nurse at Columbia HCA.

As John looks back on his careers, he sees how knowing where he fit into the big picture benefited him financially and professionally. He was able to perform his job, excel at it, and pursue additional responsibilities and roles. His knowledge of how his positions were a part of a big picture gave him confidence knowing his actions were important to the success of his organization.

As John fades to sleep, he remembers another museum exhibit he and Sharon visited on their last trip to Italy. It was showcasing some of the Italian Masters' initial sketches for major works of art. He remembers how impressed he was with the amount of detail and effort put into what would become Renaissance masterpieces. He wondered if Edvard Munch's The Scream would be as haunting if the artist did not sketch out his idea first. John did not know every step in the artistic process, but he did know it involved many layers that are built upon each other until the artist's vision is realized.

He remembered studying Leonardo da Vinci's Mona Lisa, and he realized that a company is very similar to a painting. Both a company and a painting are constructed of layers upon layers of increasingly detailed work which result in the final product. While a work of art is not made with a single pencil stroke, it is an important first step. As layers are added over the initial pencil strokes, any issues would be magnified when looking at the painting or business as a whole.

The Toonalution of John Stanley

An employee's perception of a company is created by four major influences: the workspace in which they work, the communication they receive from management, the tasks they are given to complete and the guidelines within which they are required to operate. Each of these influences their perception of how they fit within the company's "big picture" and how valuable of an asset they are to the company. If the employee is not nurtured in their workspace, communicated to effectively, assigned relevant tasks or given proper guidelines in which to work, then they will not feel important as a contributor to the company's success.

The workspace in which employees work can often affect their morale, thereby influencing their perception of how they fit within the company's big picture. While most managers would like to believe that they nurture a positive, productive working environment, often the opposite can be true. The source of negative feelings towards an employer is not always the fault of the immediate supervisor, but it can be.

Many offices are comprised of employees whose careers have spanned a variety of time periods and consist of both positive and negative experiences. The memory of these experiences over time often becomes either positive or negative, while, in reality, they were more complex in nature. An employee who remembers their experiences as negative will probably become bitter and an obstacle to their own success, while an employee who remembers the positive experiences will want to continue to be a productive asset to the company's success.

In an office environment, an employee with a negative attitude can spread their negativity to other employees thereby lowering morale. This "morale cancer" will continue to spread from cube to cube and office to office unless someone takes action against it. These employees can be identified by their "can't do" attitude.

The opposite of this is true as well. An employee with "infectious optimism" can influence the morale of an office in a positive way. These employees with a "can do" attitude will help nurture a positive attitude in surrounding employees as long as it is based on sound business principles. The asset value of an employee such as this is immeasurable and should be valued and recognized by their company.

But, if these "can do" employees only speak in generic, uplifting terms without recognizing the challenges their coworkers face daily, they will not have any substantial credibility and should be considered a liability to the company's success. A more appropriate attitude to look for in an employee would be "can do, and here are the ways we will do it."

The second factor that impacts an employee's perception of a company is the communications they receive. These communications occur through both formal and informal channels such as through emails, phone calls, meetings, water cooler conversations or the ever-present office grapevine. No matter what the source is, it is important that the management team continually communicates its goals, strategies and expectations to the employees. Rampant speculation or gossip should be addressed quickly to minimize the negative affects they will have on employee morale. The clearer the communication path is, the more secure an employee will feel towards his place in the big picture. Everyone works better when they know what is expected of them and are given the proper tools to succeed.

The third way an employee's perception is formed is by the tasks they are given to complete. The more mundane the task, the less the employee will have invested in the company's success. A challenging environment creates excitement and competition that will increase productivity and results. An employee who does not want to be challenged is an employee who does not want to grow and is content in maintaining the status quo. While it is unrealistic that every employee will have a challenging and fulfilling role, it is important to communicate the importance of all tasks to the success of the company.

The fourth, and last way an employee's perceptions are impacted, is by the guidelines within which they are required to operate. Often, companies become overburdened with self-policing policies that add unnecessary complexity and strain to the employees they were designed to help. The larger the company, the more challenging it may be to get a job done in a timely manner. The smaller the company, the faster implementation can occur but with an increase in potential risk without protective policies put in place. Remember, big businesses do not create policies without cause. Often, corporate policies are created in response to negative situations that impacted the company financially.

For example, an employee at a bakery may complain about having to wear goggles, gloves, earplugs, overalls, and a hairnet on the production floor. But these practices were put in place to help guarantee the quality of the product and to protect the employee from harm. And they were probably done over time as a response to either a lawsuit or government regulation enacted in response to an injured employee or consumer. These actions add complexity and cost to a company's ability to operate.

These perceptions form the world in which employees work and are often only one small part of a much bigger picture of the company as a whole. It is very easy for an employee, office or division to become disillusioned with the path the company is taking just through the building of false perceptions of the world which they work. At times, they can feel that their world, their part of the big picture, is falling apart around them. They can feel that their actions are inconsequential to the success of the company they work for when, in fact, they are an integral part to its success. They just do not realize how their actions impact the company.

To show how everyone has a part to play within an organization no matter how big the company or how small the task, we will compare a person's standing in their company, in the "big picture," to the creation of an artistic illustration. It is with this understanding of where employees fit in that will help them succeed and become more integral to the success of their company. It will also show how every stroke of an artist's hand to create a work of art is just as important as an employee's computer keystroke to the success of their company.

An illustration is constructed of many layers which interact with each other to form the final "picture." Like an illustration, a company is constructed of many layers which interact with each other to form the final "company." To show this, we will compare and contrast the six layers present within both an illustration and a company. These layers are titled:

1) Begin with a Vision
2) Broad Strokes Only
3) Paint, Photography, Charcoal or Clay?
4) Sharpen Your Pencil
5) Pull Out the Paint
6) Finishing Touches

Layer #1 – Begin with a Vision

No artistic endeavor begins without a vision of what the artist wants the final product to be. Sometimes this process is very clear cut, other times it is a more organic process that evolves over time. Caravaggio wanted to capture Paul's moment of conversion by painting the Conversion on the Way to Damascus in 1601, Claude Monet completed a series of paintings in 1894 of the Rouen Cathedral in his quest to study the effects of weather and light on a static subject, Auguste Rodin sculpted The Thinker in 1902 to represent Dante in front of the Gates of Hell pondering his poem, The Divine Comedy; and Frank Lloyd Wright's desire to design a dwelling that was integrated into its surroundings led to the construction of Falling Water in Southwestern Pennsylvania for the Kaufmann family in 1934.

A more recent example would be the glasswork of Dale Chihuly. He orchestrates a staff of artists to give form to his visions which range from single hand-blown globes to integrated experiences where hundreds of glass objects are woven throughout botanical landscapes.

Sometime the "art" is more about the process than the final result. Jackson Pollock was famous for his "Drip" painting between 1947 and 1950. He eventually stopped titling his paintings and assigned numerical values to them so the viewer would appreciate them as an artistic event, not as a painting depicting an identifiable subject. In 1991, Christo famously opened umbrellas over 12 miles in Japan and 16 miles in California simultaneously in an attempt to include the viewer as a participant in the artist's vision.

Each artist created iconic works of art that superseded the medium used because their vision was realized and appreciated by their intended audience. But in each of these examples, the first step was the same, to have a vision. They had to answer the question, "What do I want to create?" For our visual example, my artistic vision is to create a humorous self-portrait that pays tribute to some of my influences and incorporates my own evolution (Toonalution) into a cartoon character.

For a business to begin, it must have a vision as well. This is commonly stated as a company's "Vision and Purpose" and can usually be found in its mission statement and posted on the company's website. It must answer the question, "What do we want to create?" More specifically, "What do we want to do and why do we want to do it?" It is meant to help provide guidance to the company during its strategic decision-making processes. Like the initial step for an artist, this vision is not yet realized; it is only understood in generalities. The details will not be "penciled in" until a later layer.

An example of this can be found on Google's website. The largest internet search engine states that their mission is "to organize the world's information and make it universally accessible and useful." Notice that at this point we do not know how they are going to do this, where they will be located what departments or how many employees they will need.

Layer #2 – Broad Strokes Only

Everything, whether it is painting a landscape, building a business, or creating a product, must start with the creation of a basic structure upon which everything else will be built. This is the most important layer because a tiny mistake at the beginning of the process will be magnified as additional layers are added. It could ruin an artist's vision or cripple a company's ability to operate effectively. A stray pencil stroke and Mona Lisa's smile would not be as haunting. A business culture built on false practices brought down energy behemoth Enron. Every layer of the process, like every level of a company, adds to the final product.

Once an artist has a vision, they progress onto the next layer which is to construct the initial sketch. For our example, the artist would use broad strokes and loosely sketch his vision on paper. This might be done as a thumbnail sketch to lay out the form as well as the positive and negative spaces. General shapes are visible but you would have trouble identifying the subject. This framework keeps future additions in line and congruent with the overall goal. Reference our illustration to the left. Can you tell what the subject matter is? Probably not, but you should be able to tell where certain shapes are placed.

For a company, basic departments are created which will allow it to progress to the next layer. For most companies this would be the creation of the compliance and legal department that frames the rules of the business for employees. Or it may be the infrastructure of computer systems that allow the organization to effectively communicate. Or it might be the accounting department that allows for payments to be received and payroll to be processed. The "initial sketch" is the foundation that benefits the entire organization in that it allows it to work in a productive way that is designed to accomplish its vision.

How might your role in this part of the "big picture" feel unnecessary? As an employee in a department that deals with compliance or data processing, you might find yourself behind a computer screen or under a pile of paperwork and unable to see the value you add. This value could be keeping employees paid on time or maintaining compliance with government regulations. In both examples, the work done keeps the employees happy and the company operating in accordance with the applicable rules and regulations. Without your involvement, the company, and the employees, would be open to risk that could jeopardize its ability to operate.

Layer #3 – Paint, Photography, Charcoal or Clay?

Once an artist has his vision of what he wants to create and the initial idea captured in broad strokes, he has to decide which medium to use. Common artistic mediums include paint, photography, charcoal, clay, graphite or wood. Once a medium is chosen, the artist will then have to choose the tools for the task. For example, a painter will have to choose between different types of paint (acrylics, oils, watercolor) and brushes (natural, synthetic, sable, bristle). A photographer will have to choose between different types of cameras and lens as well as film and processing options. The options are as endless as the artist's imagination. My artistic mentor, Brian Stelfreeze of Gaijin Studios outside of Atlanta, once told me that he would use warm oatmeal if it would give him the desired effect he envisioned.

For our visual example, I've chosen Bristol board, pen and ink as the medium. This was chosen because it will complement the other illustrations throughout the book and because I'm better versed in this medium than I am in paint, charcoal, clay or photography.

For a company, the medium options are not as endless but there are many from which to choose. The medium would answer the question, "In what way do you want your business to go to market?" For a retail company, product could be transported through a customer's warehouse or the company could transport it directly to the retailer. For a customer service company, communication may flow through an online only portal or with "feet on the ground" calling on customers face-to-face. For a service company, work may be handled internally or contracted out to local providers. This choice is largely cost driven and influenced by the economic indicators and technological advancements present at the time.

Once the business "medium" is decided, the next step is to identify the tools that will be needed. Like a painter with his palette covered with acrylics of many hues, a business will need to fill its palette with the right tools to realize its vision. A retail company may need a logistics department, a customer service company may need call operators or a service company may need a team of skilled professionals.

How might your role in this part of the organization feel unnecessary? A warehouse foreman or truck driver may feel their position functions only as a storage or transportation role. A salesman or customer service operator may feel that their position only addresses immediate needs or issues and not the strategic scope they might desire. A contractor may see his work as just another job and just another paycheck.

However, all of these positions have direct interactions, with the company's customers. These positions become the face of the company to the customers they are spending millions of dollars pursuing. These are the relationships, be it sometimes in the form of brief interactions, that impact the company's customers just as effectively as any advertisement or marketing endeavor.

Layer #4 – Sharpen Your Pencil

The fourth layer is to take the initial sketch captured in broad strokes and to add details to it. This layer gives form and definition to the sketch. More details are added that give clarity to the form and tightens up the artist's vision. The form with the positive and negative spaces transforms from shapes and figures into the subject of the artist's vision.

Take a look at the figure below. Are you able to make out what the subject is? This layer expands on and adds details to the image sketched in Layer #2. Areas for shadows are identified, background structures are laid out, physical features are put into focus and the initial sketch is cemented into a stronger form. At this point, the subject should be easily identifiable as well as any supporting structures.

For the company, this expansion adds details which might include the implementation of a Human Resource, Administrative or Information Technology department. These departments give additional information on how the company is to operate going forward. They take the original structure and define it more clearly into actionable departments with individual goals and objectives to help the company succeed. Just as the subject of the illustration is identifiable, the functionality of the company should be apparent to the employee as well.

Someone in the Human Resources department will have this insight as they create the job descriptions prior to posting on career websites. Someone in the Administrative or IT department will have this insight from the assignments they are given to complete prior to rollout.

How might your role in this part of the organization feel unnecessary? A role in one of these departments is one that is far from the end product or end user. A Human Resource Specialist, Administrative Assistant or IT Technician does not talk to the customer or is involved in the creation of a product. But these roles ensure that employees are hired, managers stay on task and communication paths and operational tools remain open and functioning.

All are important responsibilities to the success of a company.

Layer #5 – Pull Out the Paint

Once the detailed sketch is complete, the artist begins to work with the final medium using the tools identified earlier. The sketch identifies what to illustrate where and it is up to the artist to execute his plan. This is the point at which the previous layers become a work of art.

Take a look at our self-portrait example. The detailed sketch has been rendered on Bristol board with pen and ink. This is the layer that gives the illustration real depth and clarity. It takes the detailed sketch and takes it to the next level of artistic realization. At this point, the work of art could be called finished because it is complete enough to stand on its own without explanation of what its purpose is. But, if the artist's vision is not realized, if it is not complete in his eyes, it is not yet finished. It will not be a success until it receives its finishing touches.

For a company this would be the ramp up and opening on the first day of business. This would include the staffing and training of new employees, the implementation of a marketing and advertising strategy and the manufacturing of goods. And, like the illustration, the company can stand on its own without needing anything additional. It can open its doors and begin to do business because it has all of the necessary departments to operate successfully. A retail company would open its door inviting customers to come in and buy its products. A customer service company would "go live" and begin fielding customers calls and addressing their issues. A service company would also "go live" and hire out its team of skilled professionals to call on its customers.

How might your role in this part of the organization feel unnecessary? Positions that deal with the implementation of a company's vision are often fast-paced and de-

manding. Because of this, they usually do not lack excitement for the employees as they see their contributions to the company's success daily. But once the newness of the role diminishes, the implementation roles become ongoing roles that can become monotonous like any other position.

Layer #6 – Finishing Touches

The sixth and final layer is to add highlights and details which will bring attention to what the artist wants the audience to see. Take a look at the completed illustration to the left. What is different about this illustration as compared to our last example? More negative spaces and hatch marks were added to give the illustration more depth and form. Notice how the black negative spaces loosely frame my arms, head and sketch pad? This was done as a way to draw your eyes to the desired areas allowing the subject to come to the forefront.

Additional issues were addressed such as adding a pencil to the first cartoon within a cartoon rendering. White highlights and a dot on its "i" were added to the Sharpie pen and the pages of the sketch pad were further delineated to separate it from the black desk.

Was it necessary to provide this extra level of detail to understand what the subject of the drawing is? No, but it was necessary in order for the artist to fulfill his vision. Without it, it would be an unfinished piece of art, a failure in the artist's eyes. My vision was to create a self-portrait that was humorous and captured my Toonalution into a stick figure. On all accounts, I'd call it a success.

Just like the illustration, this last step is not absolutely necessary to allow the company to operate profitably. But it is needed in order for the original vision and purpose to be realized. What finishing touches would a company enact as a way to realize their vision? It all depends on the original vision statement.

In our vision statement example, I identified that Google's mission was "to organize the world's information and make it universally accessible and useful." Google employs around 20,000 employees worldwide and processes over 150 million search requests daily. Its creators' wealth is valued at over $30 billion and their search engine operates in 177 countries and translates into 126 languages. Their stock opened at $85.00/share with its Initial Public Offering (IPO) in August of 2004 and it has traded as high as $747.24/share. As of 2010, the company was worth over $32 billion. On all financial measures, Google is a tremendously successful company that will remain the leading internet search engine for years to come. But is its vision realized? Not by a long shot.

While Google has assimilated a lot of data, organizing 100% of the world's information is a vision that will never be realized as new discoveries are made and world events occur. Today's headlines are tomorrow's history lessons.

As for the second part of their vision, making that information accessible and useful to everyone is another incredible feat. There are significant obstacles that exist just from a technological standpoint. As of 2010, only around 21% of the world's population is internet users. From an accessibility standpoint, the facts do not become any less daunting. Many countries are struggling to maintain electrical, sewage and transportation infrastructures much less internet connectivity.

Even if Google were to solve those issues, they would still have significant obstacles to overcome. There are an estimated 7,000 different languages in the world that have been documented. That number goes much higher if you include the different dialects present in different geographies. Google has translated only 1.8% of the world's languages. Granted, that 1.8% probably represents 80% of the world's population, but their vision has not been realized.

To help visualize Layer #6 with a more applicable example, let's look at a locally owned restaurant and see how their layers were built into a business. Their layers would begin with their vision in Layer #1 up to the actual operation of the business in Layer #5.

1) Begin with a Vision – to own and operate a successful restaurant that caters to the local clientele and seasonal tourism demands

2) Broad Strokes Only – identify a need for an Accounting, Payroll, HR and Buying departments (for a small business, these responsibilities may be handled by just a few people as the demands are less)

3) Paint, Photography, Charcoal or Clay? – will go into business as a diner

open 24 hours and offering an extensive menu including breakfast anytime

4) Sharpen Your Pencil – design menus, source ingredients, set up IT systems (cash registers), identify and define job responsibilities

5) Pull Out the Paint - hire and train cooks/waiters/hostess/cashiers, advertise grand opening, open for business, begin daily operations

6) Finishing Touches – make adjustments to the staff, menu, operating hours and other factors to increase chances for success

Up to this point, things are working fine. The diner is open, operating, serving customers and bringing in revenue. What would take it to the next level? What finishing touches can be added in Layer #6 that allows the vision to be realized? Remember, the vision was to be a "successful restaurant that caters to the local clientele and seasonal tourism demands." Up to this point, it is a restaurant that, if profitable, could be considered successful. But the vision is not realized to its fullest potential yet. What could be done to realize the vision completely? Below are a few suggestions.

To address the local clientele:

- Offer "Locals Only" specials that bring in local customers during tourism season
- Implement a points program that rewards loyal customers
- Sponsor local events
- Advertise through local celebrities and/or organizations

To address the seasonal tourism demands:

- Add additional staff to accommodate an increase in customer traffic
- Incorporate tourism themes into the menu offerings
- Offer menu items that reflect the demographic of the tourist population
- Incorporate advertising into tourism brochures

These are just a few ideas our restaurant can implement in order to realize their vision. But the final decision will have to be made by the owners. They will have to leverage their knowledge of their customer base with the cost associated with the implementation of new practices. Often, Layer #6 involves additional costs which is why many businesses, especially small businesses, do not go much beyond Layer #5.

For a large company, one option to achieve Layer #6 would be to invest in efforts that either target a specific demographic or is in a creative direction different from its traditional advertising and/or marketing plan. If the company wished to attract women more, they could sponsor a female sporting organization such as the LPGA or a female athlete. To attract young males, the company could sponsor a surfing contest, incorporate their logo into a high profile video game launch or give a product away at a rock concert. If the company wished to project a "greener" image, they could set up a volunteer day where employees are given the day off to participate in green events. If successful, the additional costs involved would be offset by an increase in visibility which will lead to an increase in sales and eventually profit. All of these are examples of a company going beyond what is needed to operate to realize their vision.

Many of these "Finishing Touches" are what could be considered something that is a "nice to have" but not a "gotta have." A company has to have certain departments in place to function daily such as an accounting department to process payroll. They do not have to support the local bowling league, sponsor a charity golf outing or offer an employee program for charitable giving.

If your company does offer "Finishing Touches" such as these, be thankful. These efforts are evidence that upper management is looking beyond the daily operations of the company and attempting to realize their vision for the company. Don't become upset if your company rejects your request to sponsor your child's little league baseball team. There is only so much money available for "Finishing Touches." Companies must make sure that it is utilized in the most effective manner. If you cannot identify an increase in revenue as a result of your sponsorship request, it will not be approved. While it may improve the company's image in your town or city, there could be a more impactful use for the resources that could be seen by a much larger audience.

What happens to employees who do not know where they fit in the "Big Picture"? This lack of knowledge can lead to distrust, confusion, envy of others and a lower morale. Many times this distrust is not present immediately, but once planted it is nurtured and grows in an unchecked environment. Do not let this happen to you because you do not understand your role.

So, where do you fit in the "Big Picture"? What Layer of the painting do you belong to? If you are not sure, have a conversation with your manager. Ask them to describe the importance of what you do, and, in effect, what he does, to the success of the company. If you are not satisfied with his answer, ask elsewhere within your department. This knowledge should not be more than one or two persons removed from you.

Once you understand your place, ask yourself, "Am I content in my role within the 'Big Picture'?" If you are content, reference Toonalution #11 to see how you can continue being an asset in a static role. If you are not content, you can do one of two things. You can own your role or you can do something about it.

If you are not content, but you are unable to change because of personal or financial reasons, then you need to own it. To do this, you must rededicate yourself to doing the best job you can possibly do with a positive attitude every day. If you cannot find enjoyment in what you do, others probably do not enjoy working with you. You risk being labeled as an unhappy and/or disgruntled employee. As downsizing initiatives occur, you will be seen less as an asset and more as a liability.

If you are not content in your role and want something more, Toonalution #2 will help identify the right career path for you. If you learn nothing else from this book, learn that it is never too late to change your career path to pursue something you truly enjoy doing. It is not the employee's job to understand the "Big Picture" but instead to own his or her part with the knowledge that it contributes to the success of the company and is necessary.

The Changing Vision

Now that you understand the importance of knowing where you fit within your company's "Big Picture," it is important to understand how your "Big Picture" may change over time. Sometimes this change is so drastic it no longer resembles the original vision as seen by the artist or the owner of a company. A drastic change is usually in response to unforeseen factors or out of necessity.

For an artist, this can be seen as a work of art that ages over time. Damage will occur as a result of how it is maintained over the years either in storage, on display or during transport. Sculptures can crack, paintings will lighten when exposed to sunlight and photographs can become stained or discolored because of their chemical compositions. An example of this is Alexandros of Antioch's Venus de Milo. Since she was discovered in 1820 by a peasant in the Aegean islands, she has been admired as a work of art despite the fact she was missing her arms. It is believed that one arm rested on her leg and the other held an apple. I prefer to let my imagination fill in the blanks on what her arms were really holding.

She occupies a place in the Louvre even though she does not represent the artist's initial vision. Time, poor handling and mounts of dirt changed her into something that no longer represents the artist's vision. Despite this, she is appreciated by millions of visitors every year.

Sometimes, an effort to restore a work of art to its original form is undertaken. This is done in an attempt to recapture an artist's vision. But, no matter how well it is done, it will never be successful because the restorer can only speculate what the artist's vision was.

For a company, this example of a change in vision occurs over time as well. Since you cannot drop or scratch a company, the damage done occurs in other ways. Competition, product quality, consumption trends, changing demographics and technology advancements: there are many factors that could negatively affect a company and change it from its original vision.

In 2008, IBM sold off its personal computer division to China's Lenovo as a way to transition from selling commodity products to selling service, software and high-end computers. It was unable to keep the division operating as a profitable asset. For a company that sold approximately 70% of the computers in 1960, this was a big departure.

Another way a company may change in response to new challenges is to change the way they go about doing business. To change the "medium" they use as seen in Layer #3 - Paint, Photography, Charcoal or Clay? The most obvious, and concerning, is the outsourcing of entire departments to other countries with a less expensive labor pool.

You may be asking yourself, if I am so important in my company's "Big Picture," how come my entire department was just outsourced to India? That is a great question without any comforting answers available. While you are important to the company as an employee, your role is even more important.

Do not become disillusioned thinking that because you are a great employee, you are immune to outsourcing. You are not. As more companies become adept at performing roles that are traditionally located in the US, the more roles that will move overseas unless operating costs are lowered. Even if operating costs were acceptable, the company may still move jobs because of the savings involved.

How does this relate to our painting example? In most cases, the quality of the company will decline as the value of the employee is diminished through practices such as outsourcing. Every company should weigh the financial savings against the loss of skilled and talented local employees. Unfortunately, as more companies become comfortable with outsourcing and financial challenges threaten their ability to realize a profit, this trend will continue.

Practices such as outsourcing will impact a company's vision by no longer reflecting the founder's vision. It may become a faux version of itself. A classic example of this can be seen in the Superman comic book. A scientist wished to make a duplicate Superman to help double his effectiveness as a hero. But the duplication machine created a faux Superman, a Bizarro Superman. This Bizarro Superman attempted to be the best Superman he could be, but he always came up short of expectations because, at his core, he was inferior to the original. A business needs to be wary of outsourcing itself until it becomes a Bizarro version of itself.

What would have happened if Leonardo da Vinci outsourced the Mona Lisa to other artists? He would end up with a Mona Lisa, but not the one he had envisioned. No matter how detailed of a description he could give, the person doing the work would not have his vision and would translate it into something that spoke to them. She might end up looking like Mona Lisa, but she wouldn't have the vitality, warmth or curious smile envisioned by her master artist.

These changes are made out of a desire to be successful or out of necessity to survive as intact as possible. The more adept a company is to making changes, the more successful they will be. But they may end up a distorted version of their initial selves.

What are some of the hard truths to knowing where you fit within an organization? The first truth is that you are expendable. This is a truth no one wants to hear. We all feel like we are so important to the company that there is no way it could ever survive without us. We do not want to come to terms with ourselves that our contributions to the company can be provided by someone else. We feel the company owes us a debt of gratitude and that they cannot ever eliminate our position. No matter how hard of a worker you are, this will never be the case. The decision-makers are purposely removed from having this level of interaction so that their decisions will be based on what is best for the long-term success of the company. Not what is best for "this guy I know in the Scranton branch."

When I say we are expendable, my statement is not limited to hourly workers or lower salary-graded employees. Everyone, from the CEO to the clerk in the mailroom is expendable. It all comes down to which employees, managers or divisions are making more money than it costs to pay for them. But understanding where you fit in the big picture will help you identify potential future risks of employment within your company.

To quote Winston Churchill, "It's not enough that we do our best; sometimes we have to do what's required." Please try to remember this if you find yourself struggling with either understanding or accepting your place within the "Big Picture." We do not always like where we end up, but how we act once we are there speaks volumes to our character, personality and moral standards.

So, what can you do today to understand how your role fits within the organization? Reference organizational charts and ask yourself, how does my job impact others within the company? How would the company be affected without my role? How would it be affected without my division? If you still do not know how your role fits within the organization, ask questions of your manager and if need be, your manager's manager. No one should question your motives. If anything, they will be encouraged that you care more about your standing within the company.

John wakes up as the airplane hits the tarmac in Tokyo. It is 11:30 PM and they are due to meet Jennifer, Aaron and Samantha at the New Sanno hotel downtown. A two-day tour is on the agenda before they are scheduled to take the train to Misowa. As they head toward the baggage claim, John notices the throng of Japanese businessmen scurrying for their flights to destinations unknown and wonders if they know how their jobs fit into their companies' "Big Picture." John waits for his luggage with Sharon, content to know that the only thing he has to understand in his post-retirement life is when lunch is served and when the neighborhood pool opens.

The Toonalution of ...Artistic Vision

TOONALUTION #2 - Creating Your Recipe for Success

Jason Dixon from Atlanta, GA, is pressed for time between connecting flights and searches for the food court at O'Hara for a quick meal. With a forty-five minute layover before his next flight, he doesn't have time to go elsewhere and must make do with the offerings present at Terminal Two. He quickly finds them lacking as most are fast food restaurants such as Hot Dog Express, Quiznos, McDonald's and Grab & Go. But he does see an upside to these restaurants of having lower prices and faster service than if he went to Terminal Three and ate at Wolfgang Puck, Macaroni Grill or Chili's with full service dining.

Jason orders a Deep Dish Farmer's Market Pizza Pie from Pizzeria Uno. The pizza's toppings include spinach, caramelized onions, sun-dried tomatoes, eggplant, pesto and a variety of cheeses. But he is informed that they ran out of a few key ingredients and he must make another choice. Apparently, Uno did not properly stock its kitchen pantry for the lunch rush. Jason orders a pepperoni pizza with plans to review his notes while he waits for his next flight.

Jason is flying to La Guardia for a two-day interview for a First Officer position with a regional airline. Jason has wanted to be a pilot since he was in grade school and heard the jets take off and land at a nearby Air Force Base. He built and flew his own model airplane and began flying real Cessnas during his freshman year of high school.

Jason was born in Madrid, Spain. His mother, Veronique Carter, was in the Air Force at the time and soon after he was born, they moved to Atlanta, GA. Jason graduated from High School in 2005 where he played viola as a member of the orchestra. He began his college career majoring in Aviation Management Operations. High tuition costs necessitated a move back to Atlanta where he enrolled at another college and attended flight school at a local Aviation Academy. Jason completed his college degree in July of 2010 in Aviation Administration and interned with a national airline for two months before landing his interview.

Jason puts away his notes and finishes his pepperoni pizza. Unlike his lunch, he's hoping that he will not be short on ingredients for the coming interviews. Jason knows he has the minimum requirements for the position but he doesn't know if that will be enough. With the recession impacting business and tourism travel, along with a high number of furloughed, experienced pilots, minimum requirements may not be enough. Jason hopes that the interviews will result with better success than his impromptu lunch and that he will be able to start down his desired career path as an airline pilot.

The Toonalution of Jason Dixon

Jason's first step on his career path will be a shaky one because of numerous factors, most notably, the affects of the recession on the airline industry. Like his lunch at Pizzeria Uno which was missing the ingredients for a Deep Dish Farmer's Market Pizza Pie, Jason found himself not sure if he has all of the right ingredients for the position he desires. Jason realized an important fact that everyone should know: effectively managing your kitchen pantry, or your skill sets, is essential in achieving success. The right combination of ingredients is necessary for both. The right education and experience is just as important to your career as flour and eggs are to baking a cake.

Does this sound familiar to you? Do you find yourself missing a few key ingredients that would help you attain your goals and pursue your desired career path? Take the first step down your career path by making sure your "pantry" has the proper ingredients for your own recipe to success thereby increasing your "asset" value to your company. In this chapter we will look at the six steps to preparing yourself for a desired role. These steps are:

1) Pantry Management
2) Whatta Dish!
3) Simple Recipes...Simple Restaurants
4) What is Your Recipe for Success?
5) How Many Courses?
6) Get Cooking

Step #1 – Pantry Management

How do you currently manage your kitchen pantry? If you are like most people, you stock up on necessary items such as sugar, bread, cereal, and acquire additional ingredients as they are needed depending on the recipe you are trying to make. These basic ingredients can be compared to the basic skills everyone needs to have in order to survive in today's world. These would include a basic understanding of math and grammar and the ability to communicate properly. The additional cooking ingredients needed for a particular recipe relate directly to the additional professional ingredients needed for a desired career. An example of this would be acquiring additional training or education for a job such as a pharmacist, doctor, accountant, etc.

Let's continue our comparison by looking at how you would manage your pantry when you wanted to cook something more specific for dinner. The ingredients listed below are for a Family Classic Meatloaf provided by Kraft Foods:

- 1-1/2 lb. extra lean ground beef
- 1 can (10-3/4 oz.) condensed tomato soup, divided
- 1 pkg. (6 oz.) STOVE TOP Stuffing Mix for Chicken
- 1 egg, lightly beaten
- 1 onion, chopped
- 1 tsp. dried thyme leaves
- 1/4 cup chili sauce

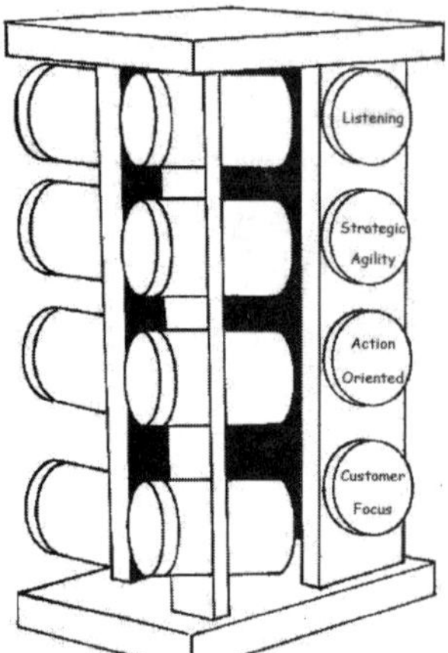

If you were making this recipe right now, would you have all of these ingredients in your pantry? Unless you do a serious amount of cooking or just came from the grocery store, you probably would not have all of them. In order to make this meal, you would have to acquire the missing ingredients prior to cooking. In doing so, you would be burdened with additional costs that are manifested in different ways. This cost might be the monetary cost involved in buying the ingredients, the time cost involved in driving to the store to get the ingredients and the cost involved just with the effort exerted. More than likely, the cost would involve all three of these.

Another cost involved may be the need for additional experience and/or knowledge to complete the task. In our recipe example, you have to ask yourself, have I ever cooked this meal before? If not, how long will it take to learn the recipe? Additionally, do you have all of the tools to make this meal? All of these questions must be answered and addressed if the recipe is to be a success.

Interestingly enough, the parameters of a career path mirror those of a recipe. The costs involved will be similar if not the same. There might be a monetary cost if you need additional schooling, a time cost involved in doing a great job and acquiring new skills and a cost involved in the effort exerted. Other similarities include the timing of certain events, attaining the proper ingredients and skill sets and identifying the approximate length of time it will take to achieve desired results. Like cooking, these parameters are not fixed and may vary depending on other unknown factors.

After you have spent the time and effort to acquire the correct ingredients, what other tools are you missing? In our cooking example, this would include utensils, pots and pans, appliances, etc. that are needed to complete the recipe. Once you have all of these, you are still not prepared to cook. Why? Because you are still missing one key ingredient that is needed for you to be successful. You need the directions explaining how to proceed forward. Without the directions, you will not achieve success because you will not know how to apply the ingredients properly. Below are the directions for cooking the Family Classic

Meatloaf from www.KraftFoods.com.

> PREHEAT oven to 350°F. Mix meat, 1/2 cup of the soup, stuffing mix, egg, onion and thyme. Press evenly into 8x4-inch loaf pan sprayed with cooking spray.
>
> BAKE 55 min.
>
> HEAT remaining soup with chili sauce in small saucepan. Spoon over meatloaf just before serving.

Without the directions, you are not likely to produce the meal as desired. You will also need directions in managing your career path. Hopefully, your manager will assist you in this endeavor. If not, Toonalution eight will cover this subject in more detail.

Now let's look at how comparing a recipe to a career path relates to Jason's situation in pursuing his first job post college. Let's assume Jason has the basic ingredients such as an understanding of math, grammar and the ability to communicate properly. What else would Jason need? Well, in order to know what ingredients are missing, you would need to know what the desired results are. In the cooking example, it was to make meatloaf. In Jason's situation, it is to be hired as an airline pilot. The job description below identifies the needed credentials and would be considered Jason's "recipe for success":

- Graduate of a four-year degree program (Postgraduate degree preferred)
- Travel documents enabling the bearer to freely exit and re-enter the U.S.
- FAA license and certification
- Minimum of 1,200 hours of total documented flight time and 1,000 hours of fixed wing turboprop or turbofan time
- Polished communication, networking and interpersonal skills
- High energy, ambition and resilience

Additional factors will be considered such as the quality of training, the complexity of aircraft flown and the types of flight operations.

Has Jason managed his "Professional Pantry" properly? Does he have the right ingredients for this position? Only Jason knows the answer to that question but it is one we should all ask ourselves when applying for a position. If he does not have all of the proper ingredients, chances are he is not going to get the position. For example, he may not have FAA licensing and certification or the minimum hours of flight time. Or he might interview against candidates who have a postgraduate degree or he might not present himself in a professional way. Would any of these prevent him from getting the job? Probably, but Jason's other ingredients might make up for a lack of experience in one area by providing more experience in another. We must keep in mind that he will be competing against other candidates who may have all of the needed credentials and extensive experience.

What ingredients are you lacking in your Professional Pantry that hinders you from pursuing your career path? Do you have all of the skills needed for your current job? What about your next position? If you do not have adequate skills for your next position, what are you doing now to address it? Are you hoping that hard work will be enough? Like it or not, hard work will only go so far in today's competitive business environment. Do not rely on it alone to realize your goals. And like an unused ingredient in a kitchen pantry, if your skill sets go unused, they will expire (go out of date). So never fool yourself into thinking that you can stop learning.

Step #2 – Whatta Dish!

So we now know it is important to keep our Professional Pantry full of the proper skill sets and experiences for our career path. But what is the recipe, what position, you are preparing for? What are you "bringing to the table" to your corporate customer? Let's take this recipe for success and career path comparison and expand it by using different types of recipes and the types of restaurants in which they would be served.

There are many different types of recipes that range from the simple to the very complex. The more complex the recipe is, the more ingredients and training will be needed to complete it successfully. For example, in *Any Idiot Can Cook with Simple Southern Recipes* cookbook, the recipe for Russell's Clam Dip is to mix one can of clams with one package of cream cheese, one grated onion and some Worcestershire sauce. Four ingredients with easy to understand instructions, it's a pretty simple recipe.

The opposite extreme would be *The Escoffier Cookbook and Guide to the Fine Art of Cookery for Connoisseurs, Chefs, Epicures*. Considered one of the premier cookbooks, it covers "everything in cookery from sauces, soups and hors d'oeuvers to roasts, poultry, game and fish, are the identical recipes used by the famous Escoffier himself, one of the greatest chefs of all time." In this cookbook, recipes are built upon other recipes which require much more skill and expertise in preparing the meal successfully.

For example, the recipe for Sole à la Daumont is shown on the next page. Additional instructions and reference recipes are captured in parentheses to show the complexity of the dish.

> "Bone the sole: severing the back-bone near the tail and the head; remove it, and leave those portions of the fillets which lie on the remaining parts of it intact. Garnish the inside with whiting forcemeat finished with crayfish butter *(recipe)*, and rearrange the fillets in such a way as to give a natural and untouched appearance to the fish. Poach *(instructions)* it on a buttered dish with one-sixth pint of white wine, the same quantity of the cooking liquor of mushrooms, and one ounce of butter cut into small lumps. Drain and cover it with Nantua sauce *(recipe)*. Place around it four mushrooms stewed in butter and garnished with crayfish tails in Nantua sauce; four small, round quenelles of whiting forcemeat with cream, garnished with truffles; and four slices of milt treated à l'anglaise *(instructions)* and fried at the last moment."

This dish is significantly more difficult to prepare than our clam dip. And with this complexity comes additional price. This price would reflect the additional cost of the ingredients, the increased skill of the chef and the general mark up present at high-end eateries for ambiance, environment and service.

So, do you want to be a clam dip or Sole à la Daumont? Put another way, do you want to be an employee who has minimal skill sets (ingredients) and experiences who settles for a minimal salary (clam dip employee)? Or, do you want to be an employee who has extensive skill sets and experiences who commands a high salary? Go for the Sole à la Daumont!

Step #3 – Simple Recipes...Simple Restaurants

Let's take this analogy a step further and compare the quality of a recipe with the quality of a restaurant. Think about what kind of establishments offer simple foods with minimal ingredients and what kind offer complex foods with complex, quality ingredients. Simple recipes, like our four-ingredient clam dip, are offered at simple restaurants such as fast food establishments like Long John Silver's, McDonalds, KFC or Arby's. While none of these has clam dip on their menus, all of their items are simple to prepare and do not have many ingredients. They offer quick, easy and inexpensive food.

These restaurants can offer inexpensive food because of the low cost of their ingredients, equipment, and staff. The ingredients are typically mass produced and arrive in frozen form. Equipment needs are minimal when compared to a full service restaurant and includes a boiler, microwave and fryer. Employee training is minimal as well, and customer service doesn't go much beyond, "You want fries with that?" Because a high school diploma is not required, most fast food chains have become one of the first employment opportunities for high school students. The only training the "chefs" need is how to operate the equipment and what's on the menu. Training would be brief. For example, McDonald's most complex menu offering is the Big Mac which has an additional bun, burger and secret sauce compared to other hamburgers available. Instead of a four step process to make, it is a six or seven step process and easily learned.

The Escoffier recipe would be found in a restaurant similar to the ones offered by the Buckhead Life Group located in Atlanta. This organization is comprised of fourteen fine dining restaurants that offer many different types of cuisine including Italian, Contemporary Parisian and Modern American dining. All of these restaurants use the best ingredients, offer thoughtful service and quality appetizers, entrees, drinks and desserts. This dining experience would command higher prices because of these amenities and their staff is paid accordingly. There would be no teenagers flipping burgers in the back. Most, if not all of the servers, hostesses and chefs would be pursuing a career in the restaurant industry and have gained their training and experience through other, more mainstream restaurants prior to joining the group.

Step #4 – What is Your Recipe for Success?

So we have two extreme examples of recipes and restaurants. But guess what? These examples can be used for employees and employers as well! The "Clam Dip" example is the entry level employee who does not have much education or experience. And it is also the company that would employ such an employee such as a fast food restaurant or retail store. This isn't meant to imply that there is something wrong with either the employee or the employer, but instead that there are different entry levels present with both. An employee who has less experience and education will apply to companies that require less experience and education for employment.

An employee with more education and/or experience will pursue a position with a company that requires more education/experience.

Our "Sole à la Daumont" example is the career employee who has a significant amount of education and experience and would be hired to work at companies that have higher requirements for employment. These could be a fine dining establishment, an architectural firm that requires a five-year degree from a prestigious college or a hospital that has internships available for medical students at the top of their class.

One of the most significant factors is understanding that your skill sets may achieve a certain position at one company but might not be adequate at another company. To help visualize this, we will add two more types of employees and companies. The first is the "Family Classic Meatloaf" recipe from earlier. This recipe takes a little more skill and number of ingredients than the clam dip but is still considered a simple recipe. This would be the employee who has some education, possibly including some college and minimal experience. It is still a fairly simple recipe but more complex than the Clam Dip. This type of company could be one that requires a college degree but it does not have to be from a prestigious university or in a specified field.

The second example is a "Chicken Marsala" recipe which is more complex than the Family Classic Meatloaf but not as difficult as Sole à la Daumont. This employee would be a college and/or MBA graduate who has the skill but minimal experience. This type of company could be one that has set a higher level of entrance, education and/or experience, for its employees. Below is a recap of the four broad categories based on the size and scope of the company. They are named from the simplest recipe to the most complex:

Clam Dip

- Employee – no experience or much education
- Company – caters to the retail industry that generally does not require employees to have a high school diploma

Family Classic Meatloaf

- Employee – some education and minimal experience
- Company – requires a high school diploma or GED equivalent

Chicken Marsala

- Employee – college and/or MBA graduate with minimal experience
- Company – requires college education and some prior experience

Sole à la Daumont

- Employee – significant amount of higher education and experience
- Company – requires a high education degree from a prestigious college and/or significant prior experience in field

These categories are intentionally vague but they capture the generalities found in the business world. Of note, the higher a company holds its standard for employment, the higher the pay scale rises. Once you have decided what type of company you want to work for, then you must answer a second question, which is what type of position do you want to achieve? Below are four different roles based on the scope of responsibilities:

- Individual Contributor – responsible for his or her own job function
- Manager – responsible for managing individual contributors and motivating employees to achieve company goals
- Director – responsible for influencing groups of managers, setting priorities and managing goals across groups
- Executive – responsible for providing strategic direction for the organization, setting company-wide goals and interfacing with the executive levels of the customer

Like the companies, the higher the level of responsibility, the higher the paycheck. Take a moment to figure out which recipe you are as an employee and which company you work for. Visualize your Professional Pantry and what your skill sets are versus the skill sets needed for a position you desire. If you have those skill sets and experiences today, congratulations! If not, identify what skills and experiences you need to be a candidate for that position. One way you can do this is by searching for the job description for the position you want on the internet. Once you find two or three examples, you can list the common skill sets and experience found in each. This is your new recipe for success. The gap present between your current education and experience and your new recipe is what we will call your "Experience Gap."

This Experience Gap is the gap you must overcome through your own efforts in gaining the additional skills to make you a qualified candidate. What skills and/or credentials do you need to bridge this "Experience Gap"? Ask your manager, your peers and others in your field who are familiar with your work. It would also behoove you to know your shortcomings. No one should ever be afraid of criticism. You will never grow if you do not know in what areas you need to improve. Take criticism for what it is, identification of possible areas of improvement. Only you will know if the opportunities ring true to what you know of your own capabilities.

Your definition for success may be vastly different from everyone else's. That is absolutely acceptable. The goal here is to assess whether or not you have the right ingredients for your Recipe for Success or what your Experience Gap is. Now that you have visualized your own career path, let's look at a few other factors.

Step #5 – How Many Courses?

If you are preparing dinner tonight, you will probably be preparing more than one course. Even the most basic meals such as a pizza, come with a second course such as a salad or garlic bread. This variety in the number of courses usually correlates with the complexity and cost of the dinner. For example, you would not have a five course bar-be-que dinner just as you would not have a one course French dinner. A more involved, challenging dinner takes more time, resources and skill to prepare properly.

Just like the number of courses in a meal, your career path will have different recipes along the way as you progress to more involved and challenging roles that take more time, resources and skill to achieve. Do you hope to become Escoffier's Sole à la Daumont? Then your career path would include the recipes for crayfish butter, Nantua sauce as well as the skills of deboning and poaching fish and preparing bread à l'anglaise. If you attempted to do the recipe without these steps, you are guaranteed to fail. This is just like an employee who takes a position he or she is unprepared for without experiencing the supporting roles.

Your career path will be one of continual learning that will include additional schooling, training or on-the-job experience. An upward moving career path must be fortified by an increase in your skill sets. You should continuously increase your experience throughout your career. If you do not, that means you are not growing or learning more and you probably will not progress beyond your current employment level. Your ingredients will go stale and you will be stuck being Clam Dip for the remainder of your career.

One key thing to remember is that you should always try to remain realistic. Do not set overly high expectations without a commitment to the process, which may take many years to complete and significant financial commitment. Factor real-world time constraints effectively so you do not become frustrated by missed timelines. Factor other significant challenges in your life such as starting a new family, moving into a new house, children going to college, etc. Do not take the 1 in 1,000,000 shot and hope for success. Take the 1 in 10,000 shot first.

As you contemplate what your experience gap is, keep in mind where you would want to work and in what role. Some hard truths will become self evident very soon. If you do not have a college degree and are applying for a position that requires one, you are not going to get the position. This is a Clam Dip employee applying for a position at a Chicken Marsala company. Conversely, if you recently completed your MBA at a prestigious university and you interview at the local McDonalds, you are overqualified and have set your goals too low. This is a Chicken Marsala employee applying at a Clam Dip company. Remember, you own your experience. Your growth is your responsibility and you need to make your goals realistic, daily, with clear goals and on a real world timetable. It is never too late to begin "cooking" your Recipe for Success!

Step #6 – Get Cooking!

So, what can you do today to become a better manager of your Professional Pantry? First, inventory your pantry. What skill sets do you currently have? What skill sets would you, your manager, co-workers and friends say are your strengths? Which ones would they say are your weaknesses or opportunities? Second, identify overall career goals with a timeline. Where do you want to be in five, ten, and fifteen years? Third, identify your "Experience Gap," what skills are needed for the next position on your career path and pursue them. Remember, it will not be easy, it will not always be fun, but it will be rewarding when you achieve what you set out to do. To review:

COOKING	CAREER
What is your recipe?	What direction do you want your career to go?
Inventory your pantry.	What credentials are you missing?
Gather ingredients.	Pursue missing credentials.
Begin cooking.	Begin your new/reinvigorated career path.

Jason Dixon leaves his interview having been offered, and accepted, the position of First Officer for the airline. He found it to be a very competitive process with thirty-three candidates interviewing for fewer than twenty positions. Jason's concerns for being out qualified were well founded as he learned that he had the second lowest flight time of all candidates. His missing ingredient, flight time, was an obstacle that he was able to overcome by being professional and projecting a positive attitude and drive to become a Captain soon. With the recent turmoil within the airline industry including the furloughing of pilots, merger of competing airlines and reduction of wages and benefits, Jason was not hindered by the negative or bitter attitude present in the more experience pilots during the interview. Jason's "the sky's the limit" attitude was seen as an asset to the airline that could spread to other pilots and staff.

With an hour layover planned in Chicago, Jason decides he will celebrate his new position by having dinner at one of the nicer restaurants found at Terminal Three. He just hopes that wherever he has dinner, that they won't be short on ingredients like he was during his interview.

The Toonalution of ...Self Development

TOONALUTION #3 - The Three-Step Selling Process of a Five-Year-Old

Tara Parker picks up the Bed, Bath and Beyond catalog and begins to search intently for a Dyson DC07 Cyclone Animal Vacuum that she feels her family desperately needs. Normally, Tara would never even consider a high dollar purchase for something as commonplace as a vacuum, but she has felt recently that the additional upfront costs would pay significant long term dividends.

Always one to do her homework, Tara's research turned up a dedicated following of the Dyson Animal Vacuum including user's blogs and websites. She found many benefits not available on other vacuums such as having an easily removable dirt canister, superior suction, HEPA filtration and a "Mini Turbine Tool" that fit her needs perfectly. She realized that it would help her clean her household more effectively and minimize allergies in the coming spring. She feels her husband of fifteen years, Rick, may be of a different opinion. Therefore, since major purchases were always made together, Tara knew she would have to sell Rick on the idea.

She patiently waited as her fifteen year old son, Bryn, and her thirteen year old, daughter, Kaitlyn, fed their animals before going to bed. Pellet sized treats from a twenty-five cent dispenser were not on the menu tonight. A buffet of processed meat chunks, poultry by-products, fish meal, grounded rice, and Timothy hay would be served to the varied customers. Feeding time at the Parker's residence has always been an event in which a can of Alpo or Meow Mix would never be enough.

As a Human Resource Specialist for the Puget Sound Veterinary Referral Center in Puyallup, Washington, it is no surprise animals migrated from her work life to her home life. While her day job includes a little bit of everything from an HR perspective such as employee liaison, hiring responsibilities, employee benefits, accounts receivable and administrative support, her home life often is much more involved with animals. Tara would like for her career path to eventually involve working with troubled teens but she has to settle for the rambunctious stray pet for now.

Not one to let an opportunity to care for a needy critter go by, Tara often acts as a foster parent to everything from abandoned cats and dogs to the fast-footed rabbit, cockatoo and even guinea pig. Her love of animals developed early and she now sees that same level of care present in both her son and daughter. Sometimes Tara wonders how they end up with one more pet than what she planned for.

Bryn, her son, being heavily involved in flag football, skateboarding, video games and math class at school, is too distracted to be much of a factor in the decision-making process. Tara's husband, Rick, begrudgingly supports the family's foray into animal husbandry but does not seek out additional tenants. Tara realized that this left her daughter as the primary subject in her critter caper.

Kaitlyn was only five-years old when Tara first witnessed her innate ability to sell. Like most salesmen, Kaitlyn knew exactly what she wanted and how to get it before she began her sales pitch. The occasion wasn't special, just a normal chilly, damp Saturday afternoon made foggy from the clouds pushing up against the Olympic Mountain Range. Her objective that day was to persuade her mother into letting her have a puppy that they were fostering until it found a new home. Her plan was to utilize known information and behavior to secure her mother's approval.

Kaitlyn did not come up with this plan by placing a lot of thought into it. She did not chart out potential strategies or success ratios. She came up with her plan by knowing her mother and how she reacts in certain situations. Tara witnessed Kaitlyn selling herself successfully. Tara realized that is what everyone needed to do in order to be successful and achieve their personal and professional goals.

The Toonalution of Tara Parker

Everyone is born with an innate ability to sell. This occurs the moment a child is born with his first cry for his mother's milk to a teenager expounding the virtues of their own cell phone with unlimited text messaging. Selling as a child evolves out of need, desire and survival. Selling as a teenager evolves out of a desire to fit in and become socially accepted. Selling as an adult evolves out of a desire to succeed and to provide for a family. While a child may never grasp the intricacies of selling, they often utilize the same basic selling techniques subconsciously to achieve desired results.

As children grow into adulthood, most lose this ability to sell as society's rules shape their perception of the world and how they should behave in it. No longer are their previous methods acceptable as they approach adulthood as they are viewed as childish and socially unacceptable. A child throwing a temper tantrum in the toy department is more acceptable than a teenager throwing a tantrum in the Apple store or an adult pouting when they do not get the raise they feel they deserve.

A child's inability to recognize their own selling abilities result in their losing those abilities without their knowledge. This does not happen to all children. Some adapt their abilities to be successful in their current situation. These groups of people are the ones often referred to as having a "natural sales ability."

As a professional, adults must tap into this repressed ability to sell themselves by highlighting their abilities and strengths as they relate to their working environment. Those who sell themselves as an asset will be viewed as more valuable to the success of their company. In doing this, they have a better chance of achieving their desired goals and being successful and thereby helping the company succeed. The results of this effort may result in a bigger bonus check, upward mobility or increased job security.

Do you sell yourself to others? Do you present your case to achieve a desired goal? Most people do not think about how they interact with others as "selling," but it is. What type of person do you think of when you hear the word "selling"? If you are like most people, you think of a sleazy, used car salesman. You know, shifty characters with greased back hair, big smile full of white teeth, plaid pants with a white belt, even whiter shoes and a pushy demeanor that puts you in self-defense mode as a consumer. Most people do not want to associate themselves with this stereotype and distance themselves from being the "selling" type. Own what it is and tailor your selling style to your needs. Redefine the stereotype!

The truth of the matter is that everyone sells everyday whether they know it or not. Think about what you did today. Did you talk to your boss about an idea of yours or express an opinion to sway a decision? You probably stated your thoughts on the matter and outlined what you thought should happen as the next steps to the process. You were selling yourself, your ideas and your desire for a particular outcome. This does not mean that you did a very good job at it, and you might have failed, but you were selling.

What about last night? If you are in a dating relationship with someone, what did you do for the evening? Did your significant other suggest dinner somewhere? Did she mention the benefits to that particular restaurant or mention she has a "buy one dinner get a second dinner of equal or lesser value free" coupon at the local Taco Hut? She, again, was selling to you. There is nothing wrong will selling to others as long as your motive is positive. Selling under false pretense or with malicious intent is not something you should ever practice as it will lead to a deterioration of trust and undermine your relationships in every aspect of your life.

Let's look back at our example with Kaitlyn. Just like in that example, most people pursue something they desire with a plan. Her plan was basic and instinctual but it was selling. To show this, we will breakout the basic steps in the selling process. Each step will be explained in further detail throughout the example. The steps are:

1. I Scream
2. You Scream
3. We All Scream for Ice Cream!

To see how this works in the real world, let's compare two scenarios. The first involving a Sales Representative trying to sell a novelty product, Sweeper Slippers "the shoes that allow you to dust while you walk" display to a store manager of a local grocery store. And the second example is a five-year old girl trying to sell her mother on letting her have an ice cream cone before dinner. Each step will compare the two examples with selling criteria and observations.

Step #1 – I Scream

A sales call is a conversation between you and the person to whom you are selling. The difference from a regular conversation is that you want both parties to share the same opinion at the end of the conversation. The first step, "I Scream," is where you present your idea along with any and all detail on how it will work and what the benefits are for the customer. Despite the title of this step, do not scream while presenting.

This first step begins when you introduce yourself and gain their interest by offering a way to address a need of theirs. By presenting your idea as a way to help them, you are ensuring you gain their attention, if only for a moment. If you put your need ahead of theirs, your selling effort may be finished before it even begins. By knowing what drives your customer, you will be able to customize your selling pitch.

You state what you want to do, why you want to do it and how it will help them. The more thorough you are in this step, the greater your chances of success will be. Show your customer that you thought out your proposition beyond addressing your needs. Have a plan that benefits both of your customer's and your own needs.

A convenient store owner may want a low priced item to bring customers inside. A retail store manager may be driven by high margins or a client may want service after the sale.

You also explain how your proposal works by identifying what the customer can expect from you. This step is where you identify or restate the benefits of your proposal. This is a great opportunity to tell the customer how you will help them. But don't oversell by setting expectations that you cannot meet. Knowing your pitch and your customer is key. If you oversell, you will hurt your chances at securing future sales.

For our Sales Rep example, he might say "Good morning Mr. Neapolitan, I'd like to get your thoughts on placing a display of our new Sweeper Slippers in the housewares department over the holiday weekend to support our 2/$5 front page ad. This will address an increase in demand as everyone prepares their house for the holidays. We would build it on Friday, merchandise it on Saturday and take it down first thing Monday morning. One sell though equals $75 in incremental sales and it will alleviate placing so much pressure on shelf inventory thereby reducing chances of having any out-of-stocks and provide an additional point of interruption to the customer."

Notice he is offering to help the manager increase sales during a demanding timeframe and sourcing adequate product thereby putting the customer's needs to the forefront.

For our Five-Year Old example, she might say, "Hey mommy, I wanna ice cream cone. You could have some too and I'll make it. It will be a lot of fun and we could do it together so you won't have to make dinner. We can have a tea party and you can watch Sesame Street with me."

In both scenarios the individual: gains the customer's attention, addresses the customer's needs and determines the customer's interest. The individual makes clear, concise statements, suggests immediate action and meets the needs of the customer. In the second example, the child is not addressing her mother's need directly. Children assume their need is the same as their parents' need. But both are serving personal needs: the sales representative to increase sales on his territory and the child, to have some ice cream for dinner.

In both scenarios the individual also: communicates anticipated results, tells who does what, when, and where, and confirms the customer understands how it works and shows how the idea satisfies a specific need. However, the child sells against herself by mentioning dinner, but she follows up with additional positive support by suggesting they spend more time together.

Step #2 – You Scream

This is the most difficult step of the selling process. This is the point where the customer has their chance to be a part of the conversation. Chances are, they will have some sort of objection to your request. Even the best salesmen will run into this situation on a regular basis.

But by being well prepared, you should be able to handle any objections the customer may have. You must anticipate what their objections may be and have a productive answer handy. Keep your options open as you may have to present a backup plan in order to secure the sale.

Sales Representative - "Our Sweeper Slippers outsell our next closest competitor, the Shoe Shamies four to one. We'll move their hutch into the backroom for the weekend. How does that sound?"

Five-Year Old - "But I wanna ice cream cone! I wanna, I wanna, I wanna!! Whaaaaaaaaaa......."

In both scenarios the individual: understands and verifies the objection, answers the objection and gains customer agreement. It is important to remember that both individuals are leveraging known information. The Sales Representative is leveraging the competitor's sales data. The Five-Year Old is leveraging knowledge of how she can influence her mother through the threat of throwing a tantrum.

Step #3 – We All Scream for Ice Cream!

This is the step where everyone gets on the same plan. You will confirm the sale and identify next steps for each party making sure expectations are understood by everyone.

Sales Representative – "So is it ok if we bring in twenty additional cases? I'll reach out to the housewares manager Friday to secure placement. I will recap our results with you on Monday. Thank you for your support."

Five-Year old – "Sniff...sniff...so, I can have some ice cream after dinner? I'll eat all of my green beans too. Thanks Mommy"

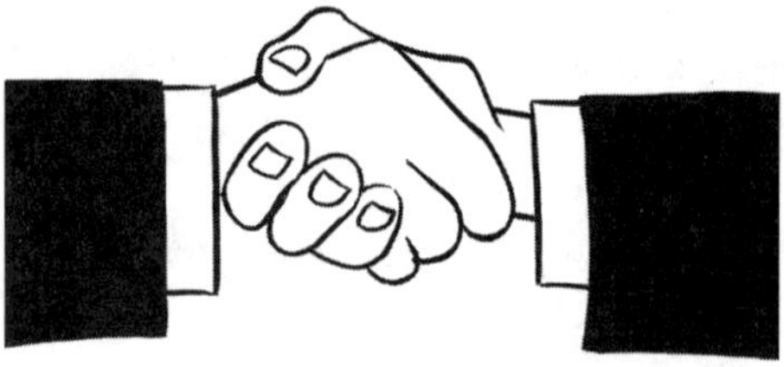

In both scenarios the individual: asks for approval to act, identifies next steps and thanks the customer.

While the child did not get exactly what she wanted, she settled for the next best thing. For the purposes of this example, I did not include the back-and-forth conversation. Always have two or three secondary goals to your original goal. This will ensure you walk away with a win, be it smaller than you wanted, but it will still be a step in the right direction.

It is important to remember a few things from this example. The first is that you should approach the selling opportunity with the needs of your customer in mind. The grocery store manager is not interested in increasing your bonus potential by moving more Sweeper Slippers, but he is interested in increasing his sales and placing the most in demand product on his sales floor for his customers. Likewise the mother is not interested in letting her child have sweets anytime she wants, but she is interested in spending time with her and seeing her eat a balanced meal.

The second is that you need to accurately identify possible objections and plan appropriate responses to overcome them. The better you are able to do this, the better your chances of success. What would have happened to the Sales Rep if the manager's objection was, "I do not want your display, I already have one on the floor (referring to the competitor)"? The Sales Rep would have walked away without selling his display. But he knew his competitor's display was on the floor and he sold against it citing sales data that would increase the manager's sales for the coming weekend. If that did not work, he would have identified other placement opportunities within the store.

This leads us into our third point to remember which is to always have secondary goals identified. For the young girl, this was ice cream after dinner; for the sales representative, it might have been a smaller display merchandised with a current display. Limit your secondary goals to no more than two or three. If you have not secured the sale after that, you are not going to get it today. Any further attempts may strain your relationship with the customer.

Lastly, and most importantly, do not let a failure to secure goal end with a negative attitude on your part. Do not pick up your ball and walk off the playground. This is sometimes difficult to do, but you cannot take a "no" personally. This will negatively affect your next selling attempt. Always be honest and straightforward as you're either always starting a new relationship or building on an existing one. One "no sale" is no reason to end what could become a fruitful relationship for both parties. The most successful Sales Representatives I have ever encountered are the ones who work hard on the relationship first and the selling second. If the customer knows you have their best interest at heart, you will not have to sell to them, they will come to you.

Everyone will have a different selling style. You will have to practice and hone your own process to achieve better results. Chances are you have a process in place right now, you just do not know it.

What are some other examples of selling that people do every day? Deciding on where you are spending Christmas this year. Negotiating which college your children will go to. Deciding on what kind of family car you will buy, the list is endless and continual. You will be selling in one form or another for the rest of your life. It wouldn't hurt to practice.

Everyone needs to recognize selling as a valuable skill applicable in both personal and professional lives. Everyone needs to sell themselves in a structured, productive way that utilizes a selling process that will address potential obstacles while not hurting their chances for success. In learning and applying this skill, many obstacles will disappear overnight.

So, what can you do today? Identify your selling style. You have one; you just do not know it yet. Compare it with the Three-Step Selling process and see where your process differs. Chances are, if you are a good seller, you are already doing a version of the process without realizing it. If you are not a good seller, learn the Three-Step Selling process and begin to use it daily. After awhile, you will see positive results. That does not mean that you will get everything you sell against. The process ensures that what you are selling is in the best interest of all parties involved. It ensures that what you are selling, whether it is an idea, a product or service, is a beneficial goal to pursue. It protects you against becoming a stereotypical sleazy salesman by forcing you to clearly identify the benefits to all involved.

Later that evening, Tara walks her two dogs, Lily, a one-eyed Pomeranian, and Mitzi, a Jack Russell mix, through their neighborhood. Cracks in the sidewalk repeat in rhythmic cadences as she leads them along the tree lined streets as she reflects on her conversation with Rick earlier in the afternoon. Tara took the Dyson opportunity to sell her idea to him by reinforcing the key benefits of buying it for the family.

Tara started the sales pitch ("I Scream") by asking how Rick's day went and stated that she felt she had an opportunity for the family. She showed how purchasing a Dyson to address their family's animal management needs would benefit the family by reducing allergies and cleaning the household more thoroughly and effectively. She supported the key benefits of having more time to spend with the family by cleaning more effectively and having fewer allergies as a result of having a deeper cleaning of the carpet, drapes and furniture. She addressed Rick's

response ("You Scream") on price by agreeing on a dollar amount that would be available during the Christmas buying season. And they both agreed on a go forward plan ("We All Scream for Ice Cream!") by securing Rick's approval to purchase the Dyson at the agreed upon price when found.

Like most skills, they improve the more you use them. Selling is no different. Today, at age thirteen, Kaitlyn has expanded her selling skills to include many more factors to increase her chances of success. Her most recent pitch, for another dog, began with research in her dog encyclopedia. Kaitlyn identified forty dogs which she liked. From there she narrowed it down to twenty by researching which dogs would do well in their living arrangement and geographical climate as well as how they interacted with other dogs and other animals.

Kaitlyn then presented this list to her mother, and asked her which ten she liked the most. From these ten, Kaitlyn further refined the list down to the final four. Needless to say, if they are asked to foster one of these four finalists, Tara would be hard pressed to let it go to another family. Pursue your own goals with a selling plan and you will succeed as well.

The Toonalution of ...Marketing & Selling

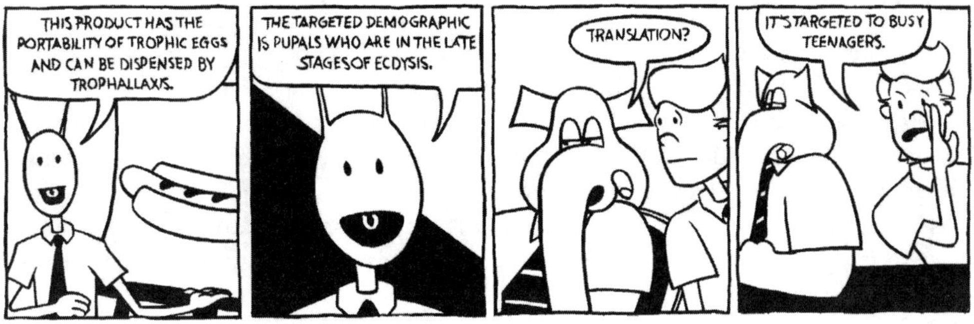

TOONALUTION #4 - Being the Must Have Employee to the Corporate Customer

In the darkness of a Monday morning, the voice of a Christian Talk Show host accompanies the flashing of 4:30 AM from Bruce Cox's digital clock waking him instantly. As he wakes, he lets his eyes adjust to the darkness as he recounts his appointments for the day. This is his daily ritual, a ritual that includes the difficult task of silently navigating his way to the master bathroom without waking his wife of twenty-three years, Kim.

Before he begins his trek, he hesitates and makes out Kim's sleeping form lying beside him. He thanks God for her, his family and for the strength he has found through his faith to deal with the recent passing of his middle son, Jonathan, who was killed in a car accident just two months after starting his first year of college. A middle child, Jonathan was a role model for his younger brother Richard and a source of pride for his older sister Maggie.

Very intelligent, full of life, a strong Christian boy and best friend to all, even to his father, Jonathan's passing has been the greatest challenge Bruce and his family ever had to confront. Through faith and friends, they slowly began to reconstruct their lives on a foundation built on the knowledge that Jonathan's short time with them was one of the greatest gifts they could ever have received. Unlike most gifts whose usefulness fades over time, Jonathan's impact on those around him continues to expand to others through a memorial scholarship fund in his name set up by the Georgia Food Industry Education Foundation.*

Bruce's feet hit the floor and a flash of discomfort wakes him as his toes wrestle his Tag Hauer watch into the carpet. As he picks it up, he remembers the occasion he received it from Kraft Foods, just one of the many perks of a career that spanned over thirty-six years in the grocery business.

Being 5'10" with a stocky build, Bruce would describe himself to others as a handsome man showing many years of wear and tear whose appearance is accentuated by "character enhancements." Only Bruce knows the origins of these "enhancements" but one would assume that they were earned by overcoming many challenges over the years.

A strong smile and stronger heart, most people would think that his forty mile drive to work at 6 AM would be to avoid Atlanta's notoriously nasty rush hour, but it is not. Bruce begins his mornings when his managers, sales force and customers begin theirs: early in the morning to get the stores ready for their consumers. His daily ritual may not be common throughout the mainstream working world, but it is very common within his world.

Bruce started his career in the grocery business at the age of twelve in a local grocery store. He earned fifteen dollars a week by walking to work from grammar school. Six years and two grocery chains later he found himself at Nabisco and eventually at Kraft Foods through an acquisition in 2001. His role is a Regional Director of Retail leading three hundred employees who manage $800 million of Kraft's volume annually. Bruce counts dealing with corporate bureaucracy as one of his major weaknesses; however he continues to succeed through his strengths which include helping employees realize their full potential, demonstrating strong leadership and by utilizing his people skills.

An hour later, Bruce finds himself waiting in line at the local donut shop with the other denizens of the breakfast on-the-go crowd. He wonders how many people are there out of choice rather than out of necessity as is his case. As he contemplates this thought, he peruses the delightful options on display beneath the florescent drenched glass case at the front of the store. All of his favorites are there: chocolate frosted donuts, apple cinnamon fritters, and almond vanilla crème horns.

Bruce thinks about what will satisfy his need at six in the morning. The lack of cash on hand and the change jingling in his pocket reminds him that a low price point is the first priority, so he decides to concentrate on the basic options and relegate the candy-enhance treats for another, more fiscally responsible time. The rumble in his stomach reminds him that something substantial is second on the list of priorities eliminating any sort of donut hole or other small portioned treat. He also would like to satisfy his sweet tooth so a bagel or muffin might not fit his need.

As he looks over the tray of glazed donuts, he notices that two of them have been smashed at some point, their frosty depressions resembling trampled snow on a dirty sidewalk. Others, on the bottom row, resemble the forgotten casseroles at an all-you-can-eat buffet a few hours before the dinner rush. Their frosted coating is cracked like the Mojave Desert baking beneath a September sun from the high intensity lights that are meant to keep them warm. There is even one donut where an opportunistic fly has gotten stuck in the glaze and is struggling for freedom against a hardening glaze offensive.

Disappointed by the current offerings, Bruce's spirits and stomach perk up when an employee retrieves a fresh tray of donuts from the oven. Dripping with warm glaze, a sweet aroma catches his senses. No contest he thinks to himself, one of these donuts will fill his need easily and save him enough money for a small cup of coffee. In a world where small was now called tall, Bruce realizes he can only afford what amounted to a mini.

Then he realizes that certain qualities present in one donut helped him choose that item over all of the other items present. As someone who has concern for his employees, Bruce realizes that the job interview for a Sales Representative position he is to conduct this morning will mirror his breakfast experience. He will choose the best candidate based on the different qualities each applicant brings to the position. How funny he finds it that a visit to the donut shop has opened his eyes to the task before him.

Bruce realizes that a job interview is a difficult event for most people. In order to be successful, the candidate has to walk a fine line between promoting what abilities they can bring to the position and promoting themselves as a person. He has conducted many interviews in the past in which the candidate failed because they put themselves ahead of his or her abilities. Bruce looks at his donut and thinks humorously that it is a good thing his interview this morning is not exactly like his breakfast experience or else the candidates will arrive covered with a sugary glaze.

The Toonalution of Bruce Cox

Once settled in his office, Bruce flipped through the resumes making sure he referenced the correct one. The first candidate was a recent college graduate with minimal sales experience. As he entered the interview room, he was shocked at what he saw. The ink-infused Chinese dragon wrapped transfixed on her neck as its forked tongue lapped at the silver dangling from her earlobe. Its purple hue bled into the collar of her rumpled blouse giving it the appearance of a mottled bruise with chance reptilian resemblance. Six silver piercings on her left ear contributed to her asymmetrical slant offsetting the other eight piercings located elsewhere on her body, visible or otherwise. Pleasantries escaped her vocabulary which was replaced by blank stares and silent reproach that did not speak to her tardiness.

Bruce wanted to end the interview here but he knew that he should go through with it. Realizing corporate etiquette overrode any of his own personal desires, he could not fathom what position she could possibly want at the company, rock band groupie aside. One thing he knew for sure: she did not project the clean-cut, positive image the company was looking for and would not be a good representative to the company's clients and customers.

Bruce began the interview with the foregone opinion that this candidate would not get the position for which she was applying. Employment in other non-customer interactive positions would hinge on availability and the applicant's ability to overcome the negative first impression given through appearance, attitude and tardiness. No matter the outcome, neither position is what she probably desires. Her career path, at least with this company, has been altered without her knowledge through both her action and inaction preparing for, and during, the interview process.

If you were the manager, would you share Bruce's feelings toward this candidate? Would you want someone who is not engaging, projects an air of aloofness, arrives late and has no respect for the company's dress code? Next, let's look at the same situation but with a candidate who is properly attired and has the right attitude.

Shelia's firm handshake accompanied her pleasant greeting and steadfast eye contact. Her engaging smile and confidence inspiring body language gave Bruce the sense that he was interviewing someone who could be his boss one day. Shelia's plain but crisp business suit exceeded the company's dress code and her attentiveness to detail was apparent immediately when she referenced Bruce's leadership ring and numerous awards on the office walls.

Pleasantries were exchanged and before Shelia had a chance to speak about her credentials Bruce had already decided she would be a great representative for the company. He was so impressed by her professionalism that he decided to shift his interview process to see what her future career aspirations may be, and if they might include a management role. Barring a complete meltdown, Shelia placed herself as a viable candidate through presenting herself appropriately and not only kept her career path secure but furthered it by being prepared.

Now that example may be a little extreme, but it gets the point across. Who would you rather be, the first applicant, or Shelia? In this example, choosing the right candidate appears obvious, but in reality it is usually not easy for the hiring manager. All factors must be considered and thought over thoroughly.

Have you ever chosen one item over another because it fit your need more completely or because it was presented in a better way? Have you ever wondered why one person succeeded where you failed? Positioning yourself as the must-have employee goes beyond having your resume printed on fancy Royal Linen Ivory White paper. It encompasses your entire being from what you wear, to what you say, to how you say it and to your attitude during the interview. This can be illustrated better by looking more closely at our donut shop example and comparing it to a job interview. To do this, we will look at the four steps in making a choice between different offerings:

1. Donut, Sausage Biscuit or Breakfast Platter?
2. Change in My Pocket or Bills in My Wallet
3. Cream-filled, Glazed or Cake
4. Eeny, Meeny, Miny, Moe...

These will seem like very easy factors to consider, and they are, but it is important that they are considered before making a decision. They will quantify the situation into three parameters: understanding the desire, understanding the costs involved and identifying the candidates so the right decision can be made.

Step #1 – Donut, Sausage Biscuit or Breakfast Platter?

Let's first take a look at what our customer, Bruce, is looking for in a donut from a need perspective. This first factor will answer the question, what need is this donut going to address? Bruce's need is to fill his empty stomach and to satisfy his sweet tooth cravings. That is it. This need could be filled with many of the offerings present at the donut shop with the exception of the bagels, croissants or breakfast sandwiches. While they would satisfy his hunger, they would not satisfy his sweet tooth.

From an employer perspective, this factor will answer the question, what need is this employee going to address? For our example, the need is to fill an open Sales Representative position. Typically, a need in the business world is very specific because it is directly related to tasks that need to be performed. A manager would not want to interview an accountant for this position just as a sale representative would not interview for a job at a law firm.

Step #2 – Change in My Pocket or Bills in My Wallet

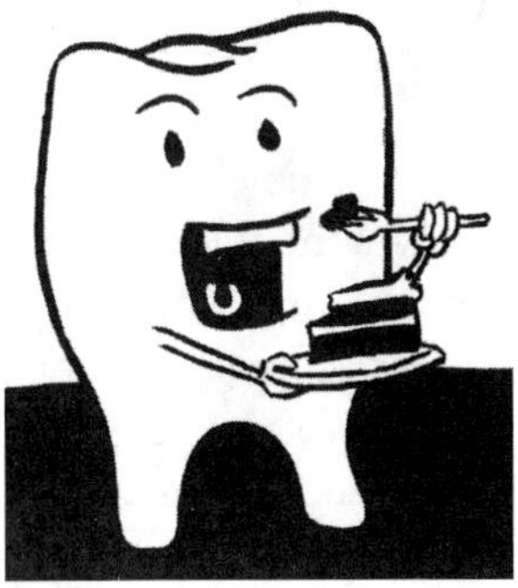

Many times, cost will eliminate many choices. This second factor will answer the question, how much do you want to spend financially? Bruce may want a Venti Non-Fat Chai Tea Latte with a pumpkin scone but finds the $7.21 price tag too steep for his breakfast budget. Similarly, an apple cinnamon fritter or a cream horn's additional expense may negate Bruce's ability to purchase a hot beverage to accompany his pastry choice. Other inexpensive alternatives such as donut holes would not address the need to satisfy Bruce's appetite.

For an employer, answering how much they want to spend would incorporate more factors than our donut shop example. These costs would vary depending on the position but they could include health and financial benefits, pension, travel budget, company car, office support or stock options. Creative organizations such as Google also provide other benefits to their employees such as lunch and dinner in their cafeteria, shuttle service to San Francisco and access to other onsite services such as an oil change station, car wash, dry cleaning, massage therapy, gym and fitness and financial classes. All of these have a cost associated to them that must be factored in as businesses address their needs and attempt to contain their operating costs. If a company offers a wonderful salary and benefits package, they have to fund the cost associated by selling additional products and/or services. If they do not do this, they will either have to cut employee's pay and benefits or risk going out of business.

Other costs factors would include the experience or potential of the desired candidate. If the candidate has many years of experience or just finished their MBA and has the perceived potential to progress upwardly within the company, they would cost more to bring on board than a high school graduate with no experience. The more education and experience an employee brings to a company, the greater they will be reimbursed financially for their efforts. This is called their asset value. Increasing your asset value to your company will be a recurring theme in this book.

Step #3 – Cream-filled, Glazed or Cake

After you have identified the need and the cost, the third factor is to identify the positive and negative attributes of the candidates prior to making a decision. Bruce has identified the need to fill his stomach and address his sweet tooth while maintaining minimal cost. At this point, Bruce's personal tastes and preferences also impact his decision.

Bruce looks at the offerings which include a variety of cake, crème filled and glazed donuts. Since he will be eating on-the-go, Bruce eliminates the filled donuts from an ease of eating standpoint. A basic cake donut may fill the hunger need and meet his price point goals but would not satisfy his sweet tooth enough. Without weighing all of the factors, Bruce will not walk out of the donut shop satisfied. Reasonably priced and in line with his tastes, Bruce feels a glazed donut would work perfectly. But which one?

If you were a glazed donut, what characteristics would you want? You would want to be fresh, eye-pleasing and you would want to address the desire. In this case, the desire is for a glazed donut because of its low price point and its flavor. What characteristics would not be appealing? You would not want an unclean appearance by being dirty or having foreign objects, such as a hair, in your glazed donut. You would not want to damage your possibility for success by having a "smashed" or "cracked" appearance; you would not want to be presented in a poor manner.

As an employer, what characteristics would you want in an employee? This would answer the question, what type of employee do you want? A positive attitude, dressed in proper business attire, timeliness to appointments and being prepared for the interview. By doing these things, you address the desire by having the right attitude, attire and attentiveness to get the interview started the right way the first time.

What characteristics would you not want? An unclean appearance, dirty complexion, unkempt hair, poorly dressed, tattoos, excessive piercings (unless appropriate for the industry) or other accessories not appropriate in a business environment or a negative attitude. Not only do these things not address the desire, they become a roadblock to making a positive impression to the interviewer.

Step #4 – Eeny, Meeny, Miny, Moe...

After you have identified the need and the cost, the fourth and final factor is to make a decision. Bruce has identified his desire, the costs parameters and the attributes of each candidate in the donut shop. He has decided on a glazed donut because it is inexpensive, fills his stomach and satisfies his sweet tooth. Bruce has three donuts to choose from: the first donut is slightly stale but has a smooth, glazed finish, the second donut's icing is still warm from the fryer and it has a delicious aroma, and the third donut has a fresh appearance but is slightly squashed in on one side. If you were Bruce, which candidate would you choose?

Bruce has also identified his desire, the costs parameters and the attributes of each candidate for the job interview. He wants a sales representative that comes at a minimal cost that fills a local territory and has potential for future roles within the company. Bruce has met two candidates and he meets with the third candidate the next day. Now he has three candidates to choose from. The first candidate, "Dragon Lady", has a college degree but was late to the interview, had a negative attitude and total disregard for corporate dress code. The second candidate has his GED equivalent, comes with 20 years of experience and is dressed in business casual attire. The third candidate, Shelia, is a college graduate, presents herself in a strong, positive way and exceeds the company's dress code policy. If you were Bruce, whom would you choose?

Remember, fitting the need goes beyond having the proper credentials. It extends to the intangibles including your attitude, body language and the way you interact during the interview. Everything communicated matters: experience, attitude, attire, etc. Success is directly related to how you separate yourself from the other candidates.

So, what can you do today to make a better impression during an interview? Follow the three A's. Adjust your Attitude to the occasion. Dress in Attire that is appropriate to the setting and increase your Attentiveness to the moment.

Be grateful for the opportunity and have fun! Your resume got you in the door; your attitude, attire and attentiveness will make the first impression. It is your business skill sets, the way you manage "your pantry" that will show how much of an asset you will be to the company. It will be the way that you sell yourself that will help you secure the position.

Why would you need to "sell yourself" during an interview? There are many reasons. There might be gaps of experience in your resume. Maybe you have some experience in a needed field but not the required time specified for the position you are seeking. You may lack the education desired for the position but may not be mandatory. How will you outsell your competitor who may have the desired education? Maybe you are the most qualified candidate but there is an internal candidate who is highly thought of within the organization. How will you outsell them? Maybe there is a glut of candidates for a desirable position or a market downturn flooded the local job market unexpectedly. Selling yourself well will help you overcome many obstacles and place you on the short list of potential hires.

You also need to remember what the employer is looking for during an interview. Think of yourself as a product for sale on a shelf in your local hardware store. What is going to stop a customer on the aisle? Most stores identify items that have a reduced price or are being promoted by a large, colorful starburst. A starburst is the star-shaped sign that highlights the benefits of a product being promoted. It identifies key data that is important to the consumer such as price, price per unit measure and amount saved.

What would your starburst be? Better put, what two or three qualities do you want to communicate during the interview?

Why two or three and not more? You only want to communicate two or three because, as with most things, people remember just a few facts. Managers are no different after an interview. And, one or two points will be made automatically by the way you present yourself, your attire and attitude during the interview. Take the time prior to the interview to identify what your starburst is. Use your experiences and skills sets to support your points and have examples ready if needed.

No matter if you are offered this position or not, do not forget to examine how you did during the interview. Self-examination will help you become better prepared for the next interview.

Later that day after the interview, Bruce stops by a local coffee shop to meet with one of his managers. As he waits for his order, he reflects on the interviews he conducted and the varying degrees of preparedness represented. The extremes were obvious to him but may not have been as obvious to the candidates. People tend to put blinders on once they get into a comfortable place and do not notice glaring omissions in the way they handle themselves with others.

The first candidate did not consciously sell herself for the job. She did not pursue her goal of employment with a well thought out plan. She failed to promote herself and her abilities. Bruce couldn't help but feel that she was oblivious to her lack of preparedness. The other candidate, though, sold herself and her skills very well, instilling Bruce with a confidence that she was the right candidate not only for the position open today, but for more demanding positions in the future.

As Bruce sits down with his employee, he notices two college kids enter who are about the same age Jonathan would be now. Just a few years older than his youngest son, Richard, Bruce silently prays for their futures and that they will be able to achieve their personal and professional goals.

** To donate send check to Georgia Food Industry Education Foundation, 1260 Winchester Pkwy. Ste. 110, Smyrna, GA 30080, Note in check memo area: Jonathan Cox Memorial Scholarship Fund. Their phone numbers are: 770-438-7744, Fax – 770-438-7761. GFIEF is a non-profit 501(c)3 deductible charity.*

The Toonalution of ...Interviewing

TOONALUTION #5 - Maintaining Functionality in the Corporate Organism

Veronique Carter is thankful for many things: her faith, her friends, her family and her career to name just a few. One thing she is especially thankful for is her health. Other than the occasional cold, Veronique has been the picture of health for the majority of her life. She has not had to undergo any type of surgery, major or minor, like most adults her age. She still has her tonsils, wisdom teeth and appendix, the organ whose Latin name probably means "useless."

Today was one of those thankful days as she reviewed her presentation before meeting with the company's stakeholders. Not one to miss a day of work because of illness, Veronique recently completed the preliminary strategy document of a 50-state filing project for her division's credit insurance portfolio that was required as a result of a large acquisition. Stakeholder buy-in is needed to progress forward and Veronique's goal for this meeting is to set expectations and timelines for each stage of the project. The enormity of the task sinks in as she enters the conference room.

Veronique's career began with an auspicious start: like most teenagers, she either didn't understand or didn't listen to the advice given to her by her parents. She decided that joining the Air Force was a safe way to leave home and to see the world. She was assigned to a "desk job" as an administrator and was able to see new parts of the world while based in Europe. Over time, she showed strong administrative and organizational skills which allowed her to excel. It was this experience that helped her successfully transition into the business world once her military assignment was over.

For the majority of her adult working life, Veronique was a single parent challenged with balancing her professional, personal and spiritual life. Even today, she seeks comfort and strength through her faith in Jesus Christ. Since her son, Jason, has started his career after recently graduating from college, Veronique has picked up a few new hobbies that have helped her manage the increasing amounts of stress present at work. Her husband, Richard whom she recently married, introduced her to fencing in 2006 which she has found to be a very enjoyable way to exercise and blow off steam. In 2007, Veronique began running in several local 10K races as training for the Peachtree Road race, a very large annual event in Atlanta. She's dreamt of completing it for many years and sprinted across the finish line in 2008.

Described by her coworkers as reliable, knowledgeable and trustworthy, Veronique is a Director of Product Filings and Compliance for AEGON Direct Marketing Services, a division of AEGON USA, and has been with the company for over four years. She has worked in the insurance industry for over twenty years and as a compliance analyst for seventeen years. She participates in the development and enhancement of insurance products in the Product Filing and Compliance department. She tracks and ensures compliance with legislative activity that affects her products so that they can be marketed and sold. Her job necessitates communicating with regulators in all fifty states as well as in Guam, the U.S. Virgin Islands and Canada.

Even with the experience and scope Veronique brings to her company, she realizes that she can only control so many of the factors that impact her at work. One of those factors is her value as an asset to the company. She has increased her asset value by continually improving her business knowledge and skill sets. She earned an Associate's Degree in Business Management from American Intercontinental University in 2002. She attends additional training classes when possible and promotes herself within her work groups through special projects or informally in her current role. As a manager, she has added value by counseling several direct reports who either expressed interest in certain areas or showed aptitude for specific tasks or projects.

While Veronique is a skilled and experienced employee, she has faced the challenges of downsizing many times during her career. In each instance, the department she worked in was targeted for reorganization. On two occasions, she was able to find work elsewhere prior to the reorganization through networking with current and past employees. During other reorganizations, her position was not targeted but she was the recipient of work that was reassigned. Each time this happened, she was able to excel in the new role as her particular job function was redefined and she was given more responsibility. Veronique believes this was possible because of her path of continual learning which has helped her adapt to change quickly.

Veronique leaves the boardroom with mixed emotions. She feels proud of her presentation because she was able to secure stakeholders' approval for the project. But her feelings are tempered by the new knowledge that the company must go through a reorganization after the acquisition to eliminate any positions or departments that have an overlay of responsibilities. She knows this is a necessary procedure as a way to maximize synergies and to reduce operating costs, but that knowledge doesn't comfort her now.

Veronique feels sick to her stomach as she faces the possibility that her department could be eliminated. She tries to rationalize reasons that the company would keep the compliance department structured the way it is for the sake of the employees, but she knows the cost/benefit ratio wouldn't make financial sense. By keeping the status quo, the company would be exposing itself to undue risk from higher operating costs and inefficiencies which would jeopardize its ability to remain competitive. Realigning and adopting best practices now would be a painful process in the short-term, but it would strengthen the company's long-term health and ability to succeed against its competitors. Veronique hopes that by making herself more of an asset to the company, by taking a preventative stance towards her career, she will remain a part of the company's future.

The Toonalution of Veronique Carter

Much like her department could become a liability to her company's future health, unproductive organs can become a liability to a human body's future health. Removal of both a department and an unproductive or troublesome organ would be a painful but beneficial for the hosts' long-term growth. In this chapter, we will discuss four similarities between how a company operates and how the human body functions. These four similarities are titled:

1. The Hip Bone's Connected to the....
2. Breathe In, Breathe Out
3. Under the Knife
4. An Apple a Day

Similarity #1 – The Hip Bone's Connected to the...

Do you remember singing the "Skeleton Bones" song as a child? The lyrics began "with the toe bone connected to the foot bone, and the foot bone connected to the leg bone...." It was a fun way for children to sing along and learn about the different parts of their body. If the song were to continue past the skeleton, it would show children that their entire body is a system of bones, organs, nerves and blood vessels that are connected and interdependent on each other to work effectively, "With the tongue connected to the throat, and the throat connected to the esophagus, and the esophagus connected to the stomach..." I've heard humorous stories where medical students used this method to help them study for their exams. Imagine hearing a medical student singing, "With the splenius capitus connected to the levator scapulas, and the levator scapulas connected to the scalenes, and the scalenes connected to the..." It might not be catchy, but it would definitely help during a medical exam.

Companies function in a similar way, but the "Skeleton Bones" song would sound more like "with the finance department connected to the compliance office, and the compliance office connected to the legal department, and the legal department connected..." Like a human body, a company functions best when all of its parts are working effectively together. And like a human body, this example can be further magnified down to the employee level. "With the Account Manager connected to the Customer Business Manager and the Customer Business Manager connected to the Customer Vice President..."

Have you ever thought of your company as though it were a human body? You probably have not, but think about it for a moment. Both a company and a human body are organisms whose parts (departments/organs) interact with each other to achieve a desired result. They both consume resources and produce byproducts in pursuit of that goal.

Companies are comprised of many smaller organizations or departments such as accounting, logistics and sales. These would be similar to the organs in a human body such as the stomach, lungs or kidneys. Just as one department in a company cannot function by itself, one organ in a human body cannot function alone. A company's accounting department could not process payroll without the sales department providing revenue. The sales department could not sell the product without the logistic department providing shipment to the customer. The company would suffer greatly and possibly go out of business if it were to close one of its departments just like a human body would suffer, or die, if it had an organ fail.

Similarity #2 – Breathe In, Breathe Out

Every breath you take is a consumption of a resource (oxygen) and every breath you exhale is an output of waste (carbon dioxide). Both a company and the human body shed unwanted, unused or unproductive parts and intake resources to help them remain healthy and productive so they may function properly and grow.

For the human body, obvious resources include necessities such as oxygen, food, water, clothing and shelter. These are resources that are needed for survival. If you are like the average person, you probably consume much more than what your body needs. I know I have more than one pair of shoes and I eat more often than I should at places that offer portions in excess of what my body requires.

Other resources include ones that are not needed for survival such as material goods, transportation, travel and leisure. These would include objects such as a designer wristwatch or purse, a new car or a vacation cruise to Alaska. They are not needed for survival, but they are resources that are consumed by all of us.

Resources that will help a human body grow would include vitamins, healthy foods, and exercise. Other resources include ones that reduce risk of harm such as safety and security equipment or lifestyle choices such as where you live, whether you smoke or not and the hobbies you have. A lifelong, beef-eating smoker whose hobbies includes cliff jumping and kite surfing will probably have a shorter lifespan than an athletic, vegetarian non-smoker who keeps his feet planted on terra firma. Ask yourself, "What type of resources do you consume?" And, "Are they beneficial to your body?"

For a company, obvious resources include materials such as paper, office supplies, computer hardware and software, transportation, fuel and other commodities that are needed for daily operations. For example, in order to keep its shelves full, a larger grocery chain would consume thousands of gallons of fuel yearly for transport of products to their stores.

Companies also intake resources that will help them grow stronger or help them face emerging challenges. These resources may be the acquisition of a smaller company that has needed assets or human equity such as talent and skills acquired through absorbing new employees.

A company and a human body also excrete byproducts as they function and grow. For the body, excreted byproducts include carbon monoxide, bodily waste, worn clothing, material goods and trash. If you have trouble visualizing your own byproducts, just try to go one week without emptying your wastebasket at home. You would be surprised how much waste even the greenest person produces. Other less obvious byproducts include how someone deals with stress or expresses his or her creativity.

For the company, excreted byproducts include daily operational waste such as office trash, vehicle emissions or food waste. It would include any industrial waste that is created from the product made by the company. For example, the steel industry produces millions of tons of sulfur, phosphorus and carbon annually as a byproduct of processing iron into steel. Less obvious waste might be lower employee moral from losing a client or environmental waste from constant travel to a customer's location. The point is that every company, just like every human being, intakes resources and excretes byproducts as a function of survival.

Similarity #3 Under the Knife

There are times when a part of the body does not work properly just as there are times when a department in a company no longer serves its function or its cost to operate outweighs the benefits it provides. What happens when this occurs to a part of the body? In extreme cases such as kidney failure, the patient may die unless he or she is placed on a dialysis machine or receives a transplant from a

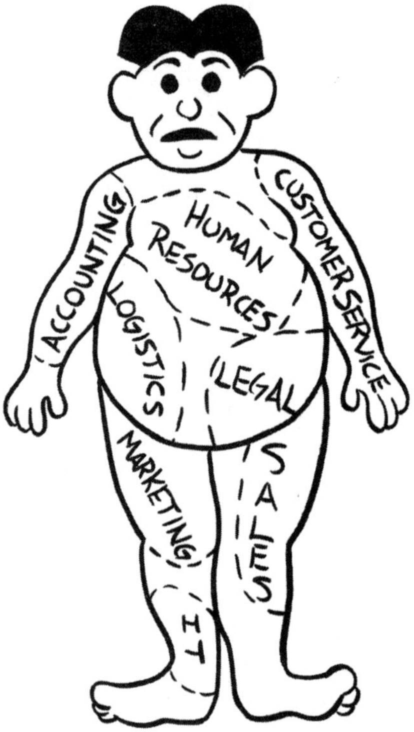

matched donor. In other, less severe cases such as the appearance of wisdom teeth, the issue may be resolved with minor out-patient surgery. Surgery is never attempted without a careful weighing of the benefits and risks involved to the patient. The doctor and his associates identify the issue, what needs to be done to address it and what hazards may arise during the procedure. It is only with this knowledge that a competent doctor proceeds with surgery.

Over time, the human body has eliminated or minimized organs which no longer add value to its long-term health. Scientists have theorized that this occurs because of changes in the environment that minimize an organ's usefulness to the host body. One example of this would be the lack of functionality found in the appendix. There is no definitive proof that explains what its function was in the past. But there are numerous scientific theories that suggest it once aided in digestion of plants for our ancestors or that it provided infection-fighting bacteria for unborn babies in their mother's womb.

Whatever its function was, today the appendix does not add value to the success and survival of the body as a whole. It is not an asset that is needed. What would be the next logical step to this process? The next step would be for the body to expel the appendix entirely to minimize the risk of infection. Most appendectomies are performed to prevent an infected appendix from rupturing, thereby endangering the surrounding organs.

As a company grows and matures, certain parts or departments of the company may not be needed anymore. Usually this is driven by technological advances such as the expansion of services onto the internet. Or it is driven by a shift in the labor force to countries such as China, Mexico or India that provide less expensive, skilled workforces. Remember, if you can perform your job from your house, someone else can perform it for less money from a house in another country. There

are many examples of this happening across many different fields including web design, accounting, payroll and animation.

While no one would elect to have an appendectomy without sound medical reasons, a company might opt for major surgery as a way of being preventative. In referencing our earlier example, what is the best case scenario of the appendix's impact on the human body? The best you could hope for would be for it to have zero impact on how the body functions. The worst case scenario would be for the appendix to burst from an untreated infection that contaminates the surrounding organs. Not only would it not contribute to the success of the entire body, but it could be the contributing factor to its demise.

What does this look like within a company? One example would be Pricing Coordinators in retail stores up until the early 1990's. These employees price marked and stocked the shelves with product in department, retail and grocery stores. This was commonly done with a manual pricing gun. Because of the frequency of price changes in advertising programs, manual pricing was needed on a monthly, weekly and sometimes daily basis. The downside to this process was the cost associated with staffing multiple Price Coordinators, the significant margin for error in pricing and the potential strained customer relations.

As computers and bar code scanners entered the mainstream, companies began to switch out their cash registers with computer registers that would scan bar codes and identify pricing through the store's computer database. Suddenly, the demand for Pricing Coordinators declined since the need to price was now obsolete.

Many Pricing Coordinators were terminated through job cuts designed to offset the cost of the new registers. One position was typically retained to handle the shelf tag transition between advertising timeframes. The "appendectomy" in this example was the removal of the pricing positions at store level. It was painful for those involved, costly to do, involved a period of recovery, but was for the long-term health of the company.

Could this have been prevented? In certain states in the northeast, it was prevented by the local unions leveraging political force to retain the positions. Pricing Coordinators continue to manually price items even today. This win only stifles progress and adds cost to the employer as well as headaches to the consumers as they deal with missing or incorrect tags and a slower checkout procedure. Another, more progressive and rewarding action would have been for the employees to learn a new trade or enhance their skills to transition to better positions within the company. This would have been the best preventative measure to take for all involved and would have ensured long-term health for the company as well as the employees.

Everyone (except perhaps Veronique) gets sick at one time or another. It isn't something we can avoid. When we do get sick, we treat the problem by addressing the issue with medicine, rest and, if needed, surgery. Minor issues require minor treatment. When you have a cold you take aspirin, drink plenty of fluids and rest. When your allergies act up you take an antibiotic or get an allergy shot at the doctor's office. But when your gall bladder or appendix becomes infected, it is surgically removed before the infection spreads to other organs affecting their ability to function.

Companies get sick as well. As with surgery, no one proceeds without a careful weighing of the benefits and risks involved to the company. Upper management identifies the issue, what needs to be done to address it and what hazards may arise during the procedure before placing any plans into action.

Like an everyday cold, these can be minor issues requiring minor treatment or they can be major issues requiring major surgery. A minor issue may be a new product that has quality issues. These minor issues would be ones that can be fixed without herculean efforts and do not have any potential to harm the consumer. A major issue could be a shift in consumer demand that was incorrectly identified which required major surgery to correct.

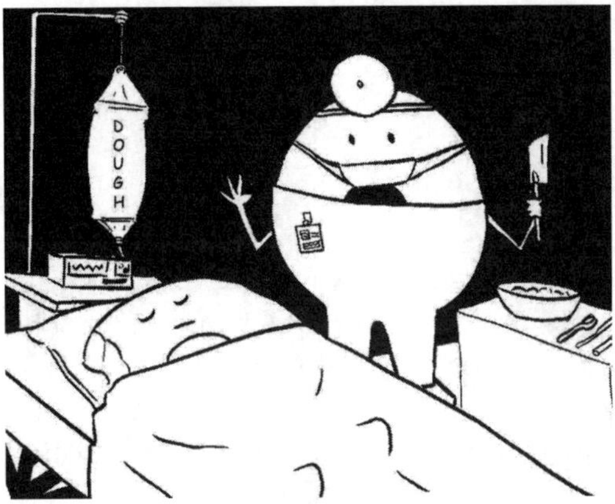

An example of this would be when Coca-Cola introduced "New Coke" in 1985. They had incorrectly identified a need to redo its classic soda formula which had become a cultural icon since its introduction in 1886. Coca-Cola executed a very costly marketing campaign to tout the "New Coke" formula but their efforts were met with intense backlash from their consumers. Coca-Cola misread its customer base and the loyalty it had to its original formula. This introduction of a new and improved product became a public relations fiasco that required major surgery to fix.

Another issue requiring "major surgery" would be when a competitor releases a new product which redefines the competitive landscape. A recent example of this is when many telecommunication companies were caught off guard by the touch features available when the iPhone was released in 2008. This example and the prior one both required major surgery for each company's survival. Coca-Cola had to bring back the original flavor introducing it again as "Coca-Cola Classic" thereby appeasing their loyal followers. The telecommunication companies had to fast-track similar touch features through their product pipeline and invest in patent fees for Apple's new technology. Both actions were necessary, costly and painful

for all of those involved. Only time will tell if their efforts were successful. But one fact is not disputable: their health would have declined greatly without intervention, possibility to the point of extinction.

We often hear of a company becoming too top heavy or unable to make changes quickly to meet the demands of the marketplace. This happens when a company becomes successful and adds layers of responsibility as it grows. Growth is cause for expansion so production can continue to meet the increases in demand, but it comes with the inherent likelihood that the company's agility will be sacrificed. Simply put, this means that instead of three or four people being the decision-makers, you now have twenty or thirty decision-makers with managers sprinkled throughout the hierarchy.

What does this mean for the company? It means that because the decision-making process takes longer, potential threats to the company's well being may not be identified until they become major issues. What once would have been minor surgery affecting a small population of employees could become major surgery affecting a larger population. This major surgery may involve downsizing or eliminating parts of the organization and require a longer healing time than what would have been needed with minor surgery. For both the human body and a company, any type of surgery, minor or major, involves procedures that are painful and require a dedicated work force which is invested in a healthy, sustainable outcome.

Similarity #4 An Apple a Day

So what do you do to minimize your chances of having major surgery? By being preventative! You can minimize health threats by utilizing the resources previously mentioned, thereby practicing "good for you" habits and by getting an annual physical and dermatology exam. You can help protect your body from harmful agents by taking vitamins and mineral supplements. You can slow down the effects of aging by applying skin lotions and minimizing your exposure to the sun. You can reduce the risk of heart disease by consuming fewer cholesterol-laden foods. You can reduce your exposure to injury by using safety equipment such as wearing your seatbelt while driving or using a helmet and pads when you ride your bicycle. The list of preventive measures is as long as the list of activities you participate in daily. Choose as if your life depends on it because in many ways it does.

The way you take care of yourself has a significant impact on your lifespan. Do you maintain a healthy or an unhealthy lifestyle? A healthy lifestyle would entail practicing "good for you" habits such as eating healthy foods, exercising regularly, drinking minimum amounts of alcohol and maintaining an active schedule. But it would also include other aspects of your life including your social life, the hobbies you enjoy, the profession you choose and where you decide to live.

An unhealthy lifestyle would entail "bad for you" habits such as smoking, drinking excessive amounts of alcohol or food and not being physically active. More extreme habits would include drug use, sexual promiscuity and participating in illegal activities.

Exposure to harmful elements can also include the profession you choose and where you decide to live. A profession that is taxing on your body will expose you to health issues that may eventually require medical intervention. You must weigh the short-term benefits against the long-term consequences. This is often hard to do in today's world where most of us live in the "here and now." Similarly, choosing to live in an unsafe neighborhood could expose you to hazardous elements that could increase the amount of stress you live with daily.

If you are like me, you fall somewhere in between the two extremes. I try to eat healthy but find myself enjoying the occasional french fries or a milkshake now and again. I have a physical and visit the dermatologist on an annual basis almost every year. I find myself playing video games when I should be playing golf. My endurance level for running long distances is not anywhere close to my endurance level for watching the Speed channel. We all have our personal challenges to overcome, but realization of our weaknesses will help us overcome them.

Will someone living a healthy lifestyle out live someone who is not? Nothing is guaranteed but statistics favor the healthy lifestyle. No one can control every factor that may impact them. The human body faces unseen challenges which can prematurely end its life such as contracting a terminal disease or being involved in an unforeseen event such as a car accident or a natural disaster.

Like the human body, a company's "lifestyle" plays a crucial role in its longevity and ability to survive. A healthy lifestyle for a company would be one where it practices "good for you" habits such as investing in its products, services and employees for long-term success. Examples of these types of investments would be better ingredients or materials for its products, additional representatives for better customer service and health and financial resources for its employees.

Other "good for you" habits would include pursuing key performance indicators

(KPIs) as measured by its investors such as organic net revenue, diluted earnings per share (EPS), operating income and margin, Stock-Based Compensation (SBC), improved working capital management, tax benefits and free cash flow.

At times some of these habits can conflict with each other. A company must invest significant resources to produce a better product, to provide superior customer service or to provide competitive health benefits or financial resources such as a 401k savings program. A company must offset these additional costs by saving money elsewhere so its financial health is strong as well. This is the critical juncture where upper management earns their paycheck. It is a balancing act that is difficult to maintain as their decisions, their go forward plan, will affect every employee, client, customer and stockholder across its entire business. Their decisions have tremendous affect on the success of the company.

An unhealthy lifestyle for a company would be one where it practices "bad for you" habits such as operating with short-term goals thereby sacrificing its long-term sustainability. Examples of this would include operating with minimal accountability, pursuit of immediate sales results or engaging in unethical practices. Unfortunate examples of this include investors losing $65 billion in the Bernie Madoff scandal in 2008, the collapse of energy giant Enron in 2001 and Nike's Asian labor practices in the 1990s.

An unhealthy lifestyle would include operating with only investors' key performance indicators in mind. Examples of this would include implementing drastic cost cutting measures to achieve a quarterly statement while sacrificing the quality of its product, services or employees. This can be a difficult cycle to break once a company finds itself practicing such behaviors. For example, sometimes a company may "load" by shipping additional product to its customers that they do not need so they achieve their quarterly objectives. But this loading will result in a slow start to the next quarter necessitating another "load" scenario. The more this is done, the harder the cycle is to break. The company will have to take a big miss in achieving its objective one quarter to fix the issue. This big miss could make it miss its yearly targets which will affect its annual financial statement and put even greater pressure on management to load again.

Like most people, most companies fall in between the two extremes. Sometimes companies swing from one lifestyle to the other based on leadership changes. Where one leader may take a hands off approach letting their managers manage their responsibilities, the next leader may do the opposite as a way to implement change and reverse negative trends.

Step back and think about what type of company you work for. Are they practicing "good for you" actions that are beneficial to its own long-term health? Or are they practicing "bad for you" habits that are not sustainable. You can be preventative in your career by not becoming complacent or static in your role. Always strive for more understanding of your organization and how your department functions within the corporate organism. Don't be the appendix! You may need to take preventative actions so that you are not a causality of the company's pursuit of short term goals. This might involve getting your college degree, your MBA or additional experience that would allow you to move to another department or company if needed.

Typically, it is difficult for your average employee to gauge whether or not their company is acting in healthy or unhealthy ways. If this happens to you, gauge whether your superiors are working with the company's long-term interest in mind. This will be much easier to identify. Are you being asked to do "bad for you" habits? If so, it is probably reflective of a culture that goes beyond your manager up all of the way to the very top of the company.

As the world marketplace continues to globalize, companies continue to adjust and adapt to be competitive in a harsh environment. Understanding current and future trends will help prevent you from becoming the appendix of your organization. Change such as this is not new and it will continue to happen. Change is not good or bad but necessary. What would happen if a company continued to fund a department that no longer provided value? What if they refused to change the way they conducted business? That department would become an illness to the organization. It would be the infected appendix that threatened the surrounding organs and the host body. Operating costs would rise, the ability to maintain a competitive edge would decline and the company could eventually face bankruptcy. Rather than one department being lost, the entire company would be endangered. As an employee, as a valuable asset, who cares about the future of your company, do not lose sight of the big picture.

There are not any companies operating today that conduct business the same way they did when they began. They have made adjustments, they adapted to not only survive, but to thrive. What are you doing to not only survive but to thrive?

As Veronique arrives home from work she tries to focus on the great job she did on her presentation and not think about what the future may hold. She wants to remain a functioning, and needed, asset to her company and prays that her preventative steps will help her do so in some capacity if not in her current role. No matter the outcome, she knows her faith, family and friends will see her through any difficult path to come.

The Toonalution of ...Organizational Agility

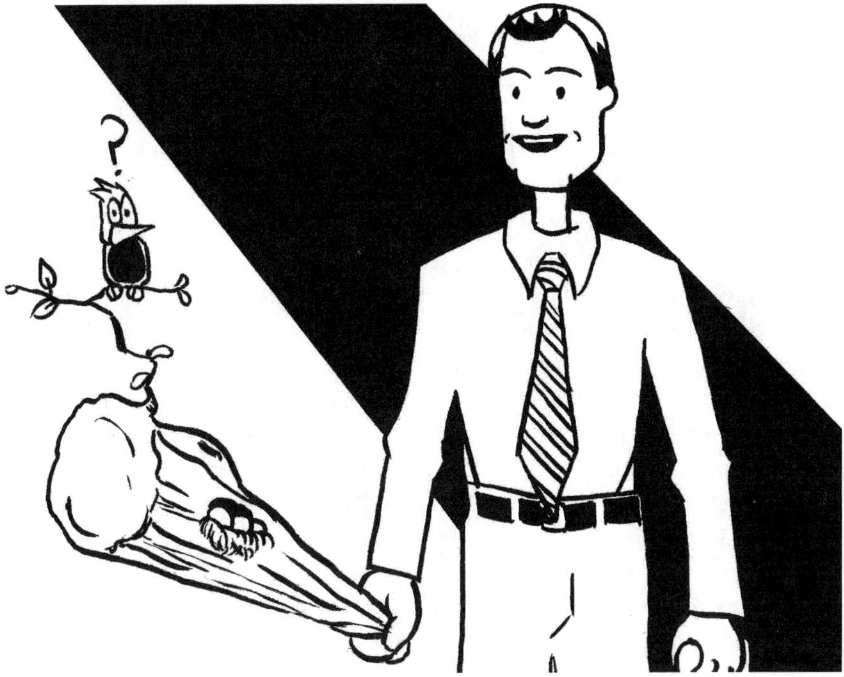

TOONALUTION #6 - Self-Assessing Your Performance Path

Greg Johns' neon green Kawasaki Ninja pops to life as he turns the ignition key. The twists of the throttle are accompanied by sporadic barks from the exhaust as it coughs out carbon buildup that accumulated in the three months since its last ride. Greg does not know much about the internal mechanics of a motorcycle, but he does know how to coax it back to life when needed. As his personal and professional lives have become more fruitful and demanding, his ride time has decreased significantly. This afternoon's ride came about because of sunny skies, cancelled conference calls, a chorus teacher wife with after-school practice and a babysitter who was swayed by an extra three dollars an hour and frozen pizza in the fridge.

Greg departs to Highway 400 towards the foothills of the north Georgia Mountains. As six lanes merge into four and then to two, Greg turns onto Highway 60 and mines his way through the gold prospecting town of Dahlonega. Once through downtown and past the "Strike 'er Rich!" tourist traps, he reaches his destination. Curvaceous, smooth, wide shoulders and debris free, Highway 129 is a siren to many adventurers in seek of a thrilling escape. She is the preferred route for motorcyclists, enthusiast car clubs and the occasional suicidal cyclist. Greg rolls on the throttle opening up the distance between himself, the motorists behind him and the stresses of his personal and professional lives.

Greg is very familiar with the stresses and demands companies are challenged with in today's corporate environment. As a consultant with over 17 years experience, Greg's insight on workforce performance was gained only after consulting with employees from many different companies and assessing their ability to perform against set expectations.

Greg graduated from Florida State University with his MBA and a Bachelor degree in Performance Management Psychology. He accepted a position as a consultant for Accenture in 1993 and moved to Atlanta to begin his career. Eventually, he decided to do the same type of consulting on his own, and in 2005 he started Optimal Workforce Performance, LLC that helps organizations, teams and individuals identify and develop strategic behaviors that lead to optimal performance. The idea of this business was formed as Greg witnessed a greater number of companies attempting to accomplish more goals with fewer resources. In order to be successful, these companies relied heavily upon increasing their employees' productivity. Greg's goal for his business is to address this need by improving a company's processes, thereby maximizing the efficiencies of their employees. He also works one-to-one with managers and executives who have increasingly less time to reinforce high-performance behaviors within their own organizations.

Greg began his business, as he describes it, after "many years of slow, agonizing contemplation and second-guessing about what (he) wanted to be when (he) grew up." Because he knew that most adults struggle with this question into retirement age, Greg's decision to act sooner than later became a turning point in his career. It not only showed him that he enjoyed his career as a workforce consultant, but that he also enjoyed the opportunities to learn and apply new skills to his business. Perhaps most importantly, he realized that if he was going to coach executives and consult organizations about changing their behavior, he needed to demonstrate change in his own behavior.

Even with these realizations, Greg still finds running his own business scary, uncomfortable, exciting and rewarding all at the same time. Because of these challenges, Greg seeks motivation through various resources. He finds short-term motivation from doing exciting work with great people. He finds mid-term motivation from helping others to improve their performance. And he finds long-term motivation from learning and applying new skills. His daily motivation, however, comes from his wife, Zelda, their daughter Eva, and his step-daughter, Cecelia. Being the only male in the house, sometimes his daily motivation revolves around being a good provider for his family. Other times, it's around finding a business associate with whom to discuss "guy topics" such as which Stooge would be the best President or which Happy Hour was better, twenty-five cent wings or dollar drafts.

As a small business owner, Greg has had to rely on one of his greatest strengths, adaptability. This strength is constantly tested and built up as he deals with different clients with varying needs and opportunities. Solution-oriented, detailed and personable, Greg has found success in unexpected situations. One example of this was when he was asked to spend three days reviewing a few business processes for a client to identify areas for improvement. His client knew he had no experience in their industry-specific processes and supporting technology. Despite this, they recognized Greg's ability to assess their company objectively and provide clear, actionable feedback.

The first thing Greg did was clarify the desired outcome, confirm his role and set realistic expectations for what could be accomplished. Given his limited experience in their industry and business processes and the limited time for the assessment, they agreed that Greg's "fresh eyes" perspective would be the greatest value in identifying quick wins to get back on track quickly.

Greg was able to build rapport with employees skeptical of his presence who wondered if he was really there to identify process improvements or to identify people who could be "downsized." They quickly felt comfortable with his presence and opened up about their past experiences with process improvement assessments. Greg helped identify improvements that saved significant time for the entire team and areas for additional follow-up that could yield even greater efficiencies. More importantly, and unexpectedly, Greg uncovered management processes and procedures that were preventing optimal performance. That three-day assessment was three years ago and Greg is now a trusted advisor to the Executive Director and continues to spend time with that organization helping them achieve sustained performance.

Greg's dream job is to travel the world with his family, play the best golf courses, and write a witty and entertaining account of his experiences. But he doesn't think the job would pay well unless he achieves some sort of notoriety. So until he either becomes a contestant on Survivor or he wrestles an escaped tiger to the ground in front of kindergarteners, he continues to shepherd organizations down the path of continual improvement.

Greg's ride on Highway 129 slows as he comes upon congestion born from an "UNDER CONSTRUCTION" sign that is framed by hard hat workers in bright orange vests. Directionally committed by concrete barriers, Greg comes to a stop and waits for the flagman to direct traffic around the site onto a temporary road. It seemed that no matter where he was going, he always had to deal with construction projects.

Even with the delay, he finds Highway 129 much more enjoyable than the secondary roads that have not been maintained properly. Those roads were often rough and treacherous to motorcyclists who were unable to enjoy the ride because they had to stay alert to remain safe. As a commuter, be it a fast, neon green one, Greg assessed the different paths available to him and chose the one that helped him achieve his goals of having a safe, exciting ride through the mountains.

Greg realized that maintaining and upgrading the infrastructure of the highway system addressed more than his or any other motorist's current needs. The roads, highways and expressways address future demands ensuring they will remain desired paths of transportation and commerce for many years to come. The ability of a road to handle transportation demands determines its desirability by motorists as a frequently taken route.

And like a road that is desired because of its ability to handle demands, Greg realizes that his business is essentially helping companies become more successful by identifying ways for them to upgrade their processes and workforce.

As he waited, Greg thought that if he were in charge of upgrading this road, he would approach it the same way he approached his business clients. He would identify the needs for improvements, design a plan to address them, project the costs of implementation and execute the plan. He would identify ways to maintain momentum while "UNDER CONSTRUCTION" and keep the project on its timetable until its completion.

This is a process he is familiar with and is surprised at how similar it is to a road construction project. He realized that the inconvenience he is being put through now is similar to the inconvenience companies go through to implement new processes. Costly and difficult while being implemented in the short-term, both will reap benefits in the future once completed.

As Greg guided his motorcycle through the construction site, he wondered what kind of "road" were most employees today. Were they newly refurbished superslabs that did not need any improvements? Or were they like the secondary roads he's discovered during his ride, two-lane and pothole ridden back roads that were hazardous. Whichever "road" an employee was, it was clear to him that everyone, including himself, needs to self-assess his or her Performance Path and decide what changes or what construction they would need to become the "road" they desired. To become the road that would increase their asset value to their company.

As Greg continues on his ride and guides his Kawasaki around the twisty roads of

North Georgia, he looks at himself in his side view mirror and takes inventory. What type of road was he? He knew a change was needed, but what?

The Toonalution of Greg Johns

The last place anyone wants to look for improvement is in a mirror. Often a source of distressing news such as darkening roots, multiplying wrinkles, migrating hair or yellowing teeth, we look at a mirror to help us assess issues on our exterior. Picking, plucking, scraping, moisturizing, implanting, applying or grooming help us address these issues. We go through great lengths to fix the issues that we can and disguised those that we cannot to present ourselves in a better light to others…figuratively and literally.

We sometimes refuse to look a little deeper to identify internal issues that may be affecting our ability to perform. We often ignore these issues instead of taking a proactive approach to addressing them.

Employees avoid their performance issues by finding easier targets such as the company they work for, their peers, management or their competition. The hardest step any employee can take is the first step towards self-improvement. But with this first step comes ownership of personal actions and results.

Ask yourself, have you lived up to the expectations you set for yourself during your initial interview for your job? Have you lived up to your own expectations of what you expect from yourself? Or are you living a life of professional complacency and false comfort? Are you looking to your company, your peers, management or your competition as reasons for your inability to perform instead of looking in a mirror at yourself? Have you self-assessed your Performance Path?

Like a road that is updated to handle increased transportation demands, as an employee, you need continual construction to remain competitive with the new superhighways being built around you. These superhighways could be the coworker in the cubicle next to you who is pursuing his MBA or it could be the new employee who was recruited out of a prestigious university or hired away from a competitor. Employees are the Avenues to Success for a company.

Employees are similar to transportation infrastructures (roads and highways) because both are fraught with shortcomings, weaknesses and are in need of extensive improvements. For a road or highway, the shortcomings could be narrow emergency lanes or inadequate access ramps and the weaknesses could be potholes or cracked pavement. The improvement could be expansion of emergency lanes and ramps or repairing potholes and cracked pavement.

For an employee, the shortcomings could be a lack of experience or education and the weaknesses could be missing skill sets that are needed. The improvements could include gaining additional experience, education or training.

Nothing is achieved without employees successfully transporting tasks from beginning to completion. Do not become a congested road that is in disrepair which damages anything that comes your way. Become a newly refreshed highway that quickly transports all tasks from beginning to end in a smooth and efficient manner.

Both a road and an employee must perform routine maintenance (construction) in order to remain competitive. If they do not, they both will face the possibility that they will become obsolete and not be used as a desired Avenue to Success.

How would you assess the condition of your Performance Path? Let's be clear, I am not talking about your Career Path. I am talking about assessing your ability to effectively do your job day in and day out: your ability to transport multiple tasks from inception to completion. The cars and trucks on your Performance Path are the tasks you are assigned as part of your job responsibilities. Some of these tasks are easy, while others take more effort to complete. At times, the volume may be light, with just a few tasks; other times it may be heavy, with many tasks needing to be completed at once. Do you have the capacity to handle this increase in the number of tasks? Or do you struggle transporting daily tasks to completion and become gridlocked in your thought process? Do you have "task traffic" that hinders your ability to be successful?

Ask yourself, how much traffic do you deal with daily? Traffic in a work environment can manifest itself in many ways. Traffic could be from an obstacle blocking your way such as a lack of experience or education. It could be congestion caused by having to transport too many tasks along your Performance Path. Or it could be a detour such as a special project or request that is beyond your position's scope of responsibility. Like traffic on a highway, traffic in your work environment will force users to look for other, faster and more convenient Avenues to Success.

How often have you found yourself stuck in traffic on a road that seems to be perpetually under construction? How many times have you cursed, silently or otherwise, the "powers that be" who make you late for your appointments? How often have you thought only about your own interests and desires rather than the end result of (eventually) enjoying an easier commute? If you are like me, this happens frequently. Sometimes when I'm stuck in a construction zone, I calculate the ratio of working employees to non-working "supervisors" and find the results frustrating.

How often do you think your manager views you as a blocked road slowing down his ability to achieve success? How often do you think of your Performance Path as a road in need of constant maintenance? How often do you think your superiors have cursed, silently or otherwise, about your performance? How often do you think your managers calculate the ratio of productive employees to non-productive employees and find themselves frustrated with the results?

How often have you found yourself mired in political or procedural "traffic" with your progress on a task? Do you need to place an "UNDER CONSTRUCTION" sign on your cubicle and begin improvements on your Performance Path today? To know whether or not you need to redo your road, to reassess your Performance Path, let's look at the different stages of a construction project:

1. Caution...Bumps Ahead
2. Which Route to Take
3. Project and Plan
4. Big Yellow Toys
5. Keep It Moving
6. Clean Up
7. Grand Opening

Stage #1 – Caution...Bumps Ahead

A caution sign placed on the side of a road is the first hint that it is in need of structural improvements before it is considered road worthy. As an employee, you do not have that kind of luxury. Currently, your "caution sign" is exhibited through the work you do as an Avenue of Success for your company. Your coworkers and manager may recognize the need for caution when assigning a task to you. But you will not recognize this need until you self-assess your own Performance Path and identify what improvements are needed to become professionally road worthy.

The first step of your self-assessment is to identify what type of road you are today. To do this, you need to take inventory of your experience, education and skill sets against your current position. By identifying what kind of road you are, you will be able to decide what kind of upgrades and improvements you will need to become the road you desire to be. For this exercise, we will review four different types of roads; New, Advanced, Average and Outdated.

The first type of road is "New," unused, without blemish and ready to take on its first commuters. While new, it is untested and it will be challenged by the demands initially placed on it. There are no potholes and the pavement has not cracked from constant use so its improvements would revolve around addressing the new demands quickly.

What kind of employee would this road be? Possibly a recent college graduate or new hire from another industry who is open to new ideas and eager to

prove themselves to their new employer. This employee is untested and will be challenged by the demands placed on him because he is either new to the working world or new to the industry. He has not been subjected to traffic by taking tasks from beginning to completion. When he is, the traffic will expose any weaknesses on his Performance Path that will need to be addressed. This onslaught of new demands will challenge his ability to remain clear of traffic.

Is this where you find yourself today? If so, brace yourself for the demands that will be placed on you and remember to address issues as they arise so you can remain a desired Avenue of Success. Identify ways to increase your ability to perform your job. By increasing your task capacity, your desirability as an Avenue of Success will increase as more tasks travel from start to finish.

The second road is an "Advanced" highway that has been successfully transporting commuters to their destination for many years. An example of this would be any of the major interstates that have complex interchanges as they intersect with other highways. Often, this webbing of roads is nicknamed by commuters such as Spaghetti Junction in Atlanta which is the northeast intersection of I-285 and I-85. This road is advanced because as commuter traffic increases, improvements are made so it remains a desired route. It is also advanced because it is the first to utilize new tools or solutions as its UNDER CONSTRUCTION projects are planned.

This proactive approach helps minimize traffic issues as the surrounding community grows. This highway needs to continually go UNDER CONSTRUCTION to make upgrades such as adding an additional lane or implementing a car pool lane as needed.

What kind of employee would this road be? This would be an employee who is proactively placing themselves UNDER CONSTRUCTION as his "task traffic" increases. He wants to remain a valuable asset to his company and seeks ways to better himself through additional education, training or experience.

Is this where you see yourself today? If so, maintain your proactive approach and continue owning your improvement plan by keeping your UNDER CONSTRUCTION sign on your cubicle. By continuing to address your road before your manager questions your ability to handle the tasks they assign you, you are showing them that you wish to remain a valued asset to the company.

And the third road is an "Average" road. This type of road has been around for a long time, has been maintained and is seen as a desired path because it is the only path. This road can be found in well established neighborhoods and business areas that are constantly used. This road is seen as an asset but is only UNDER CONSTRUCTION if absolutely necessary. These construction projects likely involve lane expansions and resurfacing to address demands and deterioration related to high traffic use. Because of this, traffic is heavy at peak demand hours and drivers would use another route if there was one available to them.

Who is this employee? Like the road, this is the "Average" employee who is competent at doing his job and shows up every day. He can be relied on to complete a task from beginning to end and he has enough experience to compensate for traffic issues. He is doing his job but does not look to upgrade his skills unless he absolutely has to. This is your employee who is "treading water" because they are doing just enough to stay afloat but are not looking to win any 100m freestyle competitions.

This employee is competent and able to address what is asked of him today but he will face challenges in the future if he does not begin a path of continual learning as demands on him increase. He will find his road becoming congested with task traffic which will inhibit his ability to complete the tasks assigned to him successfully. The pavement on his Performance Path will become cracked and small imperfections will grow into large potholes. The increasing demands will outpace his ability to keep his skill sets up to do the job without going under construction soon. Like the road, another route would be used if there was one available to the employer.

An extreme example of this can be seen at the beginning of the movie 2001: A Space Odyssey. Two cavemen clans are distraught over the appearance of a mysterious monolithic structure and begin to fight territorially over it. Based on a book written by Athur C. Clarke and adapted for the screen by Stanley Kubrick, both suggest that the monolith triggers advancement in those who encounter it. For our cavemen, it triggers an event that transitions what was a level playing field heavily in favor of one group. One caveman comes to the realization that he can use a discarded bone as a club and attacks his unarmed opponent. This use of an object as a tool to achieve a goal is not understood or acted upon by the other clan. As a result, the armed cavemen have a competitive edge over the other clan and are victorious. They smash the other clan back into the Jurassic period.

Let's transport that "tool wielding, advanced by Paleolithic standards" caveman into the cubicle next to you. Intimidated? Absolutely. In part because he smells like he just flew to work on his pterodactyl, but mostly because he could smash you back into the early 1990s to relive the Friday night antics of Balki Bartokomous and Urkel.

But this intimidation is not because of his ability to do your job as a ladder-climbing, gold-business-card-case carrying coworker. Why? Because even though he was the neatest Neanderthal around the tar pits in his day, he is hopelessly outclassed by even the most incompetent employee today.

Even a caveman from the Fred Flintstoneian era with prehistoric parrot intercoms and triceratops powered copier wouldn't be able to cope in today's business world. Why? Because the tools and processes the caveman would use would be so outdated, he wouldn't be able to perform the simplest of tasks such as composing an email, copy a document or even make coffee. From the tools he uses to his decision-making process, all are based upon obsolete needs and criteria's for success. Our caveman has not kept up with the demands around him.

The same could be said about the employee who does it their way because "it's the way I've always done it and it works for me." Soon, the tools that employee may draw upon will be outdated and they will find themselves as incompetent as a caveman.

The reason an employee from today's era is able to outperform the smartest of cavemen is because of continual learning brought about through self-assessing his Performance Path. Every new generation has more tools, more data and more resources to use as resources to do their job. As jobs become more complex and demanding, only the employees who are on a path of continual learning, the employees who are doing continued construction on their Performance Path, will remain an asset to their company. So keep your UNDER CONSTRUCTION sign handy. It will help you stay well ahead of the Joneses, or in our case, the Flintstones.

The fourth and last road is our "Outdated" road. This road has outlived its usefulness and has not been keeping pace with the needs of the area. At one time, it was the desired road of use, but as other roads were built around it and businesses and neighborhoods grew, it became secondary and as such, was not maintained properly. As potholes and cracks appeared and were not addressed, motorists chose to take a different, easier and safer route. Any car or truck that traverses this road will expose itself to financial and physical harm. This road needs significant investment just to be considered road worthy.

What type of employee would be this road? This is a stagnate employee who feels that their experience and knowledge base are sufficient for any task. They have a lot of past experiences and rely on them instead of making new ones. They are doing their job, but usually just enough to not get fired. Instead of providing solutions to new problems, they only give reasons on why they can't do something and are not open to new ideas. They are competent, but are unable to fully address what is asked of them and will not be successful in the future without a major investment. Construction is needed immediately, but the investment costs may outweigh the benefits.

An example of this can be seen with the creation of Route 66 in November of 1926. Spanning over 2,400 miles, it has been the recipient of many different nick-names including the "Mother Road", "Main Street of America", "The Great Diagonal Way" and "The Will Rogers Highway." It was created to provide a transportation route for goods and products between Chicago and Los Angeles. By 1930, it had become a competitor to the rail system by finding favor with truck drivers who preferred its flat route through more temperate climates. During the Dust Bowl of the 1930's, it was a major route for migrants who traveled west for better economic conditions, and it provided access to the west for military training bases during World War II.

Over the years Route 66 had many improvements and realignments that benefited its commuters. Its capacity and speed limits were increased, safety was improved and new routes were created around areas of congestion. Businesses such as service stations, restaurants and motor courts grew as more commuters used it. Tourism soon followed with access to the Grand Canyon and to local tourist sites such as the Meramec Caverns in Missouri. It became the site of the first drive-through restaurant and the first McDonald's as entrepreneurs found new ways to meet the needs of passing motorists.

But this success was not to last. The beginning of its end happened with the signing of the Interstate Highway Act by President Dwight Eisenhower in 1956. The first better built speedway to be created from this Act that affected Route 66 was the Will Rogers Turnpike built in 1957 that connected Tulsa with the Oklahoma-Missouri border. As other highways were constructed that ran parallel to Route 66,

or sometimes incorporated parts of it, its usefulness continued to diminish. The number of commuters decreased and, with it, the commerce that provided revenue for local businesses. It was no longer the preferred method of travel because it did not keep pace with motorist demands.

By the early 1970s, almost every section of Route 66 was bypassed by a modern highway and businesses failed and closed their doors for good. As tax revenue from tourism declined, so did road repairs and Route 66 fell into disrepair. On June 27, 1985, the last section was bypassed by Interstate 40 in Williams, Arizona and it was officially removed from the United States Highway System.

As an employee, are you in danger of becoming outdated like Route 66? If so, start your construction project today to begin making the repairs to your Performance Path to become an Avenue to Success for your company.

Stage #2 – Which Route to Take?

So which road are you? Are you a "New" road that needs minimal construction to handle the new demands placed on you? Are you the "Advanced" road that proactively addresses issues and remains the desired avenue? Are you the "Average" road that needs minimal construction to become even more successful? Or are you the "Outdated" road that is in desperate need of significant repairs just to transport commuters successfully to their final destination? Whichever road you are, you will fall into disrepair unless you perform routine maintenance.

The first avenue of choice, pun intended, meets current demand and expected growth, is able to accommodate unexpected surges in volume and is up for all challenges. This enhanced Performance Path does not have to be a highway or interstate. It just has to be ahead of the demands for the area in which it services.

As an employee, it could be a production technician who has experience as an end-user of their product; it could be an Administrative Assistant at an architecture firm who is familiar with the basic underpinnings of AutoCAD, or it could be the warehouse foreman who facilitates new employee equipment training classes.

What do these employees have in common? These are employees who keep a high standard of themselves. They are always looking for ways to improve what they do and want to continually learn better ways to do things. They are open to change and usually embrace it before their coworkers. Some of them may be motivated with aspirations of moving up within the company, others out of a high personal standard of performance. They are the Avenues to Success for their company.

Identify which route you want to take and research what it will take to get there. Will it take additional experience? Education? Both? For new employees it may be gaining initial and much needed hands-on experience. For more senior employees, it may be additional training, education or experience. If you are unable to figure this out on your own, ask for help from your manager or HR representative.

Stage #3 – Project and Plan

As a review, Stage #1 identified what kind of road you are today. Stage #2 identified what kind of road you would like to be. Stage #3 is where you identify the improvements that need to be made to become your desired road. To do this, you will design a game plan and capture all costs associated with implementation. This stage identifies what needs to be done, how it will be done, how long it will take and what resources will be needed for completion.

For a construction project, this would include developing a construction timeline, designing blueprints, gathering cost estimates from contractors, factoring the project's impact to the city, designing of temporary structures and concrete mix, reviewing quality assurance and control, sourcing material procurement and cost engineering. This is all of the pre-work that occurs before beginning the actual construction.

For you, as an employee, this would include identifying your training goals, gathering cost estimates for furthering your education, developing a timeline for completion, soliciting support for cross-training opportunities, weighing your ability to manage your other responsibilities and identifying who you will need assisting you and when.

Stage #4 – Big Yellow Toys

Once the assessment of what improvements are needed is complete, the costs are projected and the plans are ready for implementation, the fourth stage is to begin the UNDER CONSTRUCTION project. This is the stage where all of the resources are collected and put to use. Execution against the identified timeline begins, progress against set goals is assessed and adjustments are made as needed to keep the project on task. If you were running a race, this would be the firing of the starter's pistol signaling the race to begin. For our example, it would be the backfiring of a bulldozer upon start up.

For the road construction project, this would involve transporting all of the big yellow vehicles most of us would recognized from our childhood. Not made of plastic, in Japan or with "TONKA" stenciled in black on it, these full-size toys are not available at your local Megamart store. Weighing anywhere from a few thousand pounds to over 110 tons apiece, they are capable of moving millions of pounds of dirt and debris daily.

After the equipment and manpower are brought to the site, work would begin according to the identified timeline and adjustments would be made to keep the project on task. People and equipment would get dirty, commuters would be inconvenienced and events surrounding the work site would be impacted.

As an employee, this is the stage where you begin your project by starting your continue education classes, training seminars, cross-training opportunity or another avenue you identified as the right construction project to become the desired road. You would act against your designated timeline and make adjustments as issues arise.

Like the construction site, your professional and personal life would get dirty as well but in a figurative sense. You will have increased demands on your time and resources which could increase your level of stress. You and the people around you may be inconvenienced by your plan. Maybe you will not be able to go to a party with friends because you have to study, maybe your patience is less because of the increased workload you have because of a cross training opportunity, or maybe you will not be able to buy a new pair of shoes because of the cost of tuition. Be mindful of this and remember to weigh this as one of the costs to placing yourself UNDER CONSTRUCTION and make your decision accordingly.

Stage #5 – Keep It Moving

Once the UNDER CONSTRUCTION project is underway, the fifth stage is to

maintain momentum by keeping the project moving. To do this, it is important to minimize any negative situations that will affect others. By keeping these situations limited, objections to the plan will be minimized and direction and drive will be maintained towards the goal.

The best image of this is at a construction site. By minimizing traffic and keeping commuters on their routes in a quick manner, there will be fewer objections to the project. As a way to minimize this, the foreman could place signs to direct traffic down a detoured path, place flagmen to guide commuters around sensitive areas, pull up construction cones during high volume times and schedule work on one section at a time or during off-peak hours of use.

As an employee, you would want to minimize negative situations with your coworkers, spouse and family. By minimizing headaches to others, you will have fewer objections to your UNDER CONSTRUCTION project. You will help ensure that potential obstacles are eliminated, impact to others is minimized and clarity of purpose remains a priority. A big part of this will revolve around your ability to manage your time effectively. Prioritize your work and personal schedule so that the balance between your work life and your personal life is maintained

Stage #6 – Clean Up

The next to last stage of the UNDER CONSTRUCTION project is to clean up the site and ready the project for its grand opening. At our construction site, clean up would include disposing of trash, recycling waste, transporting construction equipment, sweeping dirt and debris clear, painting markers and removing barricades.

As an employee, clean up would occur after you have completed your UNDER CONSTRUCTION project. If you acquired additional education, training or work experience you would update your resume and communicate your accomplishments to management.

Cleaning up would also include working ahead as much as possible in your current position so that your manager will see an increase in your effectiveness as his employee.

Stage #7 – Grand Opening

This is the stage where your UNDER CONSTRUCTION project opens for the first time. This is when all of the hard work and sacrifice is rewarded.

At the construction site, the foreman would participate in a ribbon cutting ceremony at which local politicians pose for publicity pictures and take more credit than they deserve. The site would open allowing cars and trucks to access the new lanes or routes available. Commuters will assess the viability of this new and improved road for their needs. They will weigh the price of past inconvenience against current and future accessibility. The UNDER CONSTRUCTION project's success will reflect on the amount of time and effort put into it. If shortcuts were taken or standards were compromised, the success present at its Grand Opening may be short-lived.

As an employee, the size of your opening would depend on what your career path looked like. If your project was completed as a way to help you do your job better and improve your own work/life balance, you may be the only one invited. If you went UNDER CONSTRUCTION as a way to pursue a promotion, you need to invite many people to your opening. You could do this by sending out your updated resume or by expressing your interests to upper management.

But, just like at the construction site, your UNDER CONSTRUCTION project's success will reflect on the amount of time and effort you placed in it. Hopefully your success will be long-lived reflecting your efforts to improve your Performance Path.

What will happen if you do not begin an UNDER CONSTRUCTION project? What happens if you do not take a path of continual learning? Your "caution" sign will

become more predominate as your manager and coworkers steer important tasks to other Avenues to Success that are more reliable. The tasks assigned to you will become less frequent or harder to complete. Desire for a new employee to be hired (a new road to be built) will intensify as your abilities to facilitate tasks to completion are questioned. Ask yourself, how long will it be before your road is deemed unfit for traffic?

What are some of the benefits of placing an UNDER CONSTRUCTION sign on your cubicle? By being proactive you will become more of an asset to the company, increase your job security, minimize stress in your life and be respected by your peers. View an UNDER CONSTRUCTION sign not as an impediment to your achieving your goals but as an exclamation of continual improvement to be more successful in the future. You will be able to address future needs and develop yourself to your fullest potential.

Greg's trek through the construction zone was rough, dirty and stressful but he made it through to the newly resurface portion of Highway 129. His Ninja carves its way through Neel's Gap and over Blood Mountain to T.W.O. (Two Wheels Only), a small restaurant/motorcycle resort and campground which is cattycornered from the only gas station within twenty miles. Greg makes a quick pit stop and tops off his tank before he heads home. Normally, he would have grabbed one of T.W.O.'s pulled pork sandwiches, but he's hoping there will still be some pizza left over from the baby sitter. As he approaches the construction site, he views it not as an inconvenience to him as a commuter, but instead as an improvement project that will make his next ride on Highway 129 much more enjoyable for many years to come.

The Toonalution of ...Self-Assessing

TOONALUTION #7 - Understanding the Qualities of the Best Managers

Tom is reading a chapter about the importance of Servant-Based Leadership from Larry Burkett's book, *Business by THE Book*. But a nudge on his elbow reminds him that he is not alone. He looks down and sees his collie, Abby, resting one of her front paws on his knee, with a Frisbee in her mouth. Her expression says "serve me" as she looks mournfully out the sliding door of Tom's houseboat towards the shoreline. Her message is crystal clear; now is "Frisbee Time" and not "Tom Time."

Tom Darrow of Roswell, Georgia, is the Founder and Principal of Talent Connections, LLC and Career Spa, LLC. Talent Connections (www.talentconnections.net) is a recruiting consulting firm that was ranked by Inc. magazine as one of the fastest-growing private companies in the United States two years in a row. Talent Connections specializes in recruiting, including recruitment process outsourcing (RPO), executive search, HR consulting, and contract recruiting. Making the connections to recruit top talent is the mainstay of the company whether it's by revamping the hiring process or building a network of contract recruiters for companies to pull from at a moment's notice.

Tom's other company, Career Spa (www.careerspa.net), is one of the innovative leaders in career rejuvenation for both organizations and individuals. Comprised of nationally recognized recruiting and career transition experts, Career Spa offers a comprehensive and cost effective model for career transition services that provides best practices, one-on-one coaching, encouragement and accountability to individuals affected by corporate downsizing. Tom's team understands the challenges faced by employees who are transitioning because of downsizing and teaches the "success practices" to be mastered for an effective job search.

Tom began Talent Connections and Career Spa eleven and two years ago respectively and has been in the recruiting industry for over twenty years. He received his BBA in accounting from the University of Notre Dame. Prior to starting his own businesses, he worked as a National Recruiting Director at Accenture, a Recruiting Manager at XcelleNet and a HR and Recruiting Manager and Auditor at Price Waterhouse.

As the Principal and Founder of two different companies, Tom has looked to many different types of leaders for inspiration. He believes the foundation of good leadership begins by leading with a servant heart and integrity. He also believes leaders should be determined, futuristic and competitive as well as quality decision–makers, especially when there is a lack of data on which to base a decision. As a Fighting Irish graduate, Tom has many such leaders to look back on as inspiration. He views Lou Holtz as one of the great leaders who was effective at building a world class football team. Football heritage at Notre Dame is long and illustrious if you look back to an age prior to the coining of the term Y2K.

In 1913, Coach Jesse Harper led the Fighting Irish to an undefeated season. Legendary coach Knute Rockne revolutionized football by popularizing the use of the forward pass. His ability to leverage new tools in creative ways gave his team an edge above their competition. He guided Notre Dame through five unbeaten seasons and amassed six national championships in his thirteen year tenure which was cut short when he was tragically killed in a plane crash while en route to participate in the filming of The Spirit of Notre Dame.

Another Irish great Frank Leahy became Notre Dame's coach in 1942 and secured six undefeated seasons and five national championships. Today, Knute Rockne and Frank Leahy rank one-two as the two winningest coaches in college football history. The only other examples of successful leadership at Norte Dame where the coach led more than ten seasons would be Ara Parseghian (1964-74) and Lou Holtz (1986-1996) who both achieved winning career percentages above 0.760.

While Tom looks to others for motivation and drive, he is also motivated by his desire to serve. He finds motivation in wanting to help others by providing them the tools to achieve success, by acting in spiritually and morally just ways and to have fun by sharing his successes with his family, friends and associates. Tom always attempts to recruit a great team of people to work with him. He then serves them by providing them with the processes, tools, methodology and encouragement to help the team reach its goals. While he loves the flexibility to manage his own time, he struggles with his inability to accomplish two impossible tasks: to please everyone and to always achieve the high expectations he sets for himself.

Tom was the President of SHRM-Atlanta, the Atlanta affiliate of the Society for Human Resource Management, where he led the chapter to the most membership growth in its forty-one year history. He feels he succeeded because he was able to rally a great group of people around achieving the BHAG (Big, Hairy and Audacious Goal) that he set for them. But Tom's successes have not come without many failures in the past.

Leading with integrity and a generous spirit, one of Tom's greater strengths is his ability to lead a group to reach a desired goal. This coupled with his desire to help connect people to their vocational calling led to the creation of his businesses. He hopes in the future that he will be able to utilized his business expertise to found and operate a Christian ministry.

With two businesses to keep tabs on, Tom finds little time to read up on some best practices that other business leaders have found effective. Today, he broke away from his home office to relax on his houseboat on Lake Lanier. His wife, Anne, has joined him as well as their three dogs, Abby, Ace, and Lillie. It is Abby who is nudging his elbow to play Frisbee. Tom gives in to Abby's persistence and grabs the Frisbee from her. He decides that a happy, tired dog will allow him more time later to catch up on his reading.

As they make their way to shore, Tom wonders if he is the leader or is being led in this situation. He is doing something he doesn't necessarily want to do (play Frisbee) but with goals and motivations of his own (wear Abby out so he can have some quiet time). He looks back to the boat and sees Anne giving Ace and Lillie doggy treats. All three dogs look to them for food, fun and comfort. There isn't any leadership apparent in any of them echoing the saying that dogs have masters and cats have staff. Tom realizes that it is better to be seen as a master, the leader, by your dog than to be seen as staff, being led, by your cat. With two opposing perceptions of America's favorite pets, Tom wonders what type of leaders each would be if given the opportunity.

Instinctively, Tom knows he would not want to work for a cat. He cannot envision a cat as a manager operating with a leadership style under which he could operate. As Tom throws the Frisbee to Abby, he sees how having her as his manager would be just as unproductive as working for a cat, but for completely different reason.

Abby is like most typical dogs, eager to please and always looking for direction, scraps around the dinner table or a pat of praise on the head. Those qualities would not transfer well into a management role. As a manager, her leadership style would be lacking at best. She would look to others for direction, constantly seek praise from her employees and pursue short-term (quick) rewards. As an employee, Tom would become frustrated by not knowing what to do, get tired of affirming an incompetent leader and not have long-term job security because of her focus on short-term wins. Tom appreciates her for what she is, a loveable companion and energetic Frisbee partner.

The Toonalution of Tom Darrow

How well do you work with your manager? Do you find it difficult to remain motivated under his or her leadership style? What is your responsibility as an employee when you find yourself in this situation? Many employees, new or otherwise, struggle under the direction of their manager. Sometimes this is because of personality clashes, other times it is because they are having difficulty understanding their manager's expectations which we will cover in Toonalution #9: *Playing the Expectations Game*. But more often it is because they do not understand their manager's leadership style. By better understanding it, you will be able to work more effectively because you will know its limitations and how it affects you and your coworkers. This understanding will help you limit your exposure to negative situations and remain productive when facing challenging times. You will be able to continue on your career path and achieve your goals.

No two managers are alike. They are formed by their skill-sets and leadership styles. Some managers lead as the decision-maker, while others allow their employees to contribute as they see needed. What type of leadership style would you want to work for? All employees have a vision of what they would consider the "perfect" manager, but that vision in reality doesn't exist.

Let's explore why there are no "perfect" managers by looking at the positive and negative management traits found in common animals. We will also identify four predominant leadership styles that most employees will encounter while on their career path. By understanding the different leadership styles, you will be able to identify which style you are working under and make adjustments to help you remain motivated along your career path. We will review three lessons:

1. Cats are Curious, Ants are…
2. Dogs Have Masters, Cats Have Staff
3. Who's the Boss?

Lesson #1 – Cats are Curious, Ants are...

It has been established that Tom's dog, Abby, would not make a very good manager or leader. What kind of manager would a cat be, or other animals such as an ant, elephant, chimpanzee or panda? Why would I ask such a question? Because by understanding that different animals have different traits that affect the way they behave, you will see that different managers have different leadership styles that affect the way they manage employees. Like an owner who tries to walk her cat on a leash, not understanding how your manager leads can result in public humiliation and possible physical injury.

Everyone knows the old saying that cats are curious. It is commonly thought that cats tend to be curious and dogs tend to be loyal. Different animals have different traits associated with them. Sometimes these stereotypes are true, other times they are not. Let's look at the traits and habits of five different animals and the pros and cons their leadership style may exhibit if they became a manager.

Domestic Housecat (Felis domesticus)

Positive Traits - Cats are confident, curious, smart, crafty and playful. They jump on opportunities (mice, spiders, balls of yarn) with a killer's instinct. They eliminate vermin, provide companionship, are clean and good communicators through purring, hissing, growling, meowing or chirping.

Negative Traits – Cats are not totally domesticated and could "go wild" at anytime. They are territorial and resist attempts to be trained or led which can result in

moments of insubordination. They are not team players or customer service friendly. They clean themselves wherever and whenever they want and view their owner as a resource rather than as a leader. They can be easily distracted by catnip, string, reflective lights or fast moving shadows.

As a manager, a cat would lead with confidence, curiosity and be very opportunistic. They would thrive if they could see beyond their own needs. But their self-serving traits coupled with their disdain for teamwork would result in a disastrous leadership style. Direction would be dictated by their immediate needs and the work day would be punctuated by two hour naps on a subordinate's lap.

Lack of direction and fear would motivate employees to pursue their own agenda as an act of self-preservation. Turnover would be high and morale would be low, especially for the employee who had to change the manager's litter box.

Common Ant (Formicidae)

Positive Traits – Ants follow orders, do not question authority, and are very social. They can solve problems, carry up to fifty times their own weight and work in the interest of the overall colony or team. They operate with distinct divisions of labor and utilize non-traditional communication paths (pheromones). They can build bridges, are defensive and have a strong sense of survivability. There are billions of them; they will eat anything and are action oriented.

Negative Traits – Ants cannot think independently, work only with direction from the Queen and get distracted by sugar. Being born into their roles as a worker, soldier, drone, or queen, they have very little organization agility and are unable to work across corporate divisions. They have a view towards work that borders on fatalistic which can cloud their decision-making process.

As a manager, an ant would struggle greatly as a leader because he would only act on directions provided by his superior. This lack of personal leadership would relegate him to the role of a messenger and not a leader. He would be unable to design and execute independent initiatives. He would be very hard working and would work on a task until it reaches completion no matter the cost to him, even to the death. He would operate with a "do as I do" mantra which others may find off-putting if the task seems unrealistic or unwise.

His employees would become frustrated at this lack of leadership and inability to make decisions independently. Some employees would take advantage of the situation and not do their job knowing he would take the workload on himself. Very much a glorified employee, the respect he receives for his hard-work ethic would be overshadowed by his incompetence as a manager and leader.

African Elephant (Loxodonta africana cyclotis)

Positive Traits – Elephants remember everything, are equipped with a versatile appendage and work for peanuts. They are intelligent, thick skinned, compassionate, self-aware and have the largest brain of any animal. They are very social creatures and possess good communication skills (trumpeting and groaning) that can be heard across great distances.

Negative Traits – Elephants tend to sweat the small stuff (mice) and will charge when they feel threatened. They suffer from low self-esteem because of a lack of role models (think Dumbo) and their communication avenues can be very loud and disruptive.

As a manager, an elephant would be boisterous, social and able to build a loyal team around him. He would lead based on past relationships and experiences and utilize those memories for making future decisions.

Employees will enjoy working for an elephant manager as long as business is good. As soon as he faces a challenging environment, employees should expect him to become defensive and irritable because of his inability to work through small details. Because of a lack of role models, an elephant manager would be self-conscious about others' opinions of him which may be compensated by an extremely competitive nature. Elephants are more of a visionary than an executioner and would be better suited in an upper management role.

Common Chimpanzee (Pan troglodytes)

Positive Traits – Chimpanzees are very intelligent, able to create tools as needed and are great at multi-tasking. They can coordinate troop hunting strategies, influence others and are capable of altruistic behavior. They are good communicators, have an aptitude for photogenic memory and build trust through grooming and playing with others.

Negative Traits – Chimpanzees can be insubordinate to the troop hierarchy (management), manipulative, deceptive and territorial. The males are more aggressive than females and immature tendencies can be seen in both.

As a manager, a chimpanzee would lead with compassion, group support and with an ability to adapt to new challenges. A great team builder, a chimpanzee would be an ideal mid-level manager as they can be insubordinate and immature in dealing with office politics and upper management. At times manipulative and territorial, it is best to work for a female chimpanzee as they are less aggressive and more nurturing towards other members of the troop (team).

Employees will learn adaptability and increase their problem solving skills if they work for a chimpanzee. As a manager that operates "in the vines" with their employees, a chimpanzee will earn their respect if they can refrain from being immature or manipulative. If an employee wishes to move upward within the company, they will need to find a better mentor who is more "upper management" friendly as chimpanzees struggle with developing direct reports and political savvy. Maintaining professional composure is one of their greatest weaknesses.

Giant Panda (Ailuropoda melanoleuca)

Positive Traits - Pandas have a strong jaw, are herbivorous with a diet that consists 99% of bamboo and spend 10 to 16 hours a day eating. They are classified as a carnivore because of their digestive systems and have a "pseudo thumb" which is an elongated and enlarged wrist bone that helps them eat. They communicate through vocalization and scent marking, are adept tree climbers and rely on spatial memory instead of visual memory. Adults are generally solitary until mating season.

Negative Traits – Panda are a threatened species which are terrestrial and solitary except to mate. Pandas do not establish permanent dens, can't digest cellulose and do not have much energy because of their diet. Females are not tolerant of each other.

As a manager, pandas would rely on their communication skills to lead employees. Interaction with employees would be sparse as daily priorities would revolve around eating and sleeping. Because of their reliance on spatial memory, which is remembering the layout of one's environment such as an office space, a panda manager would be resistant to change.

Scarce in numbers, a panda manager would disappear from the office when presented with an opportunity to mate. But these occurrences would be well co-ordinated events that would be planned for in advance and involve international government coordination.

Employees can expect a minimal direction from a manager who would be absent from daily interaction with employees. This will require a work force that is self-reliant and able to work together without much, if any, intervention from management. This "paws off" management style is susceptible to being influenced by a dominate team member.

These examples showed five different animals and how their different leadership styles would affect the way they would manage their employees. Which one would you prefer to work for? It's a tough decision that isn't made any easier when you factor in the aromas associated with their hygiene and offerings provided for during office luncheons. Bananas and insubordination from the chimp? Or a "can do" attitude and road kill with the ant? I bet a cold shoulder and pizza in the break room from your manager is looking a little better to you now.

By now, hopefully you are looking at your manager in an entirely new light. And unless they are an escaped circus bear masquerading as middle management, it is in a better light. The point of this exercise was to show that all managers have positive and negative traits that affect their leadership style and thereby affect you, the employee. Learn to adapt to and overlook the bad traits and concentrate on their good traits.

Lesson #2 – Dogs Have Masters, Cats Have Staff

As mentioned earlier, there is an old saying that "dogs have masters and cats have staff." And there is a lot of truth to this saying. Both dogs and cats look to their masters for food, shelter and affection. Dogs "pay" their way by providing protection to the family even if it only manifests itself as a half-hearted bark towards a creaking floorboard. They are motivated by their own needs and desires. Whether it is a back and forth glance between its master and a ragged tennis ball, or a slow moving paw that explores the possibilities of a nap on the couch, dogs seek approval, acceptance, comfort, entertainment and security from their masters. Because of this motivation, dogs will perform tricks or complete tasks as directed by their master. They see their master as their "Alpha Dog" that provides for their needs and the needs of the pack. In the case of the domesticated dog, their pack is the rest of the family.

While dogs look to their masters for direction, companionship and praise, cats operate a little differently. They look to their "masters" as an infinite resource of food, play toys, litter and treats. Their stance is more of a "this is mine and you may use it" which lends itself to the "staff" nomenclature found in our phrase earlier. While a nudge against your leg may seem affectionate, the cat is actually marking you as a part of her territory.

Our cat, Corina, is not what you would consider a cuddly cat. More than once she has swiped at a passing toddler that did not respect her personal space. Clawless and somewhat harmless, her actions were self serving and not in the interests of the toddler. A quick cry and comfort from the toddler's mother, and they were on to less precarious objects for entertainment.

Just as cats and dogs have many differences that impact their interaction with others, all animals across the globe have different traits as well. And just like different animals have different traits, different managers have different leadership styles. It is important to understand the traits of your manager in order to be successful as an employee. To do this, we will identify five different leadership styles used by "homo sapien" managers and other examples from the animal world.

The first leadership style we will look at is Autocratic. This is a manager who operates as an authoritarian. He keeps all information close and maintains a tight hold on his employees. He is the decisions-maker and only involves those in high positions in the decision-making process. He does not see his employees as a source of valuable information; therefore he does not seek their opinions on how to proceed. As the gatekeeper, all information flows down from his position and employees are expected to do exactly as they are directed. Some of the advantages for this leadership style is that it projects confidence and consistency and provides clarity of communication. With one message from one source, employees know what direction they are going in and who is responsible for their actions as a team.

Advantageous in some regards, this leadership style does have its disadvantages as well. Because employees are not involved in the decision-making process, they may not be motivated to perform at a high level because the plan is not their plan. They are not invested in its success beyond a paycheck. Employees under this leadership style may also become dependent on their manager and lose critical decision-making skills. This will affect them as they progress along their career path because it will become an underused skill set that may need work prior to their being promoted to a leadership position.

What kinds of animals function with an autocratic leadership style? The animals with this style are the predators that hunt in packs and seek direction from an Alpha leader such as a wolf or a gorilla.

The second leadership style we will look at is Paternalistic. This style is dictatorial like the Autocratic style in that the manager makes all decisions. The distinction is that the manager's actions tend to be in the best interest of the employees and not the business as a whole. This style promotes loyalty from the employees, a sense of ownership in the success of the company and lower personnel turnover.

Some negative aspects of this style include developing employees that become dependent on direction and unable to think for themselves. Bad decisions can be made that benefit the employees but are harmful to the long-term health of the company. This can lead to employees not liking their manager because his bad decisions decrease the employees' sense of security.

What kinds of animals function with a Paternalistic leadership style? Look in the mirror. Humans are a great example. Everyone has had a parental figure or is a parent. How many parents have ridden "It's a Small World" at Disney because they loved the animatronics, smelly water and sticky seats? Not many. Parents subject themselves to overpriced admission tickets, sweaty teens in character costumes and seven-dollar sodas for their children's benefit, not for their own.

The third leadership style we will look at is Democratic. In a Democratic style, employees participate in the decision-making process. Everything is agreed upon by the majority before action takes place. Communication flows both ways from the top down and the bottom up. This style is good for complex situations because it is reliant on more than one voice, opinion or experience base, thereby opening the conversation up to new ideas and opportunities.

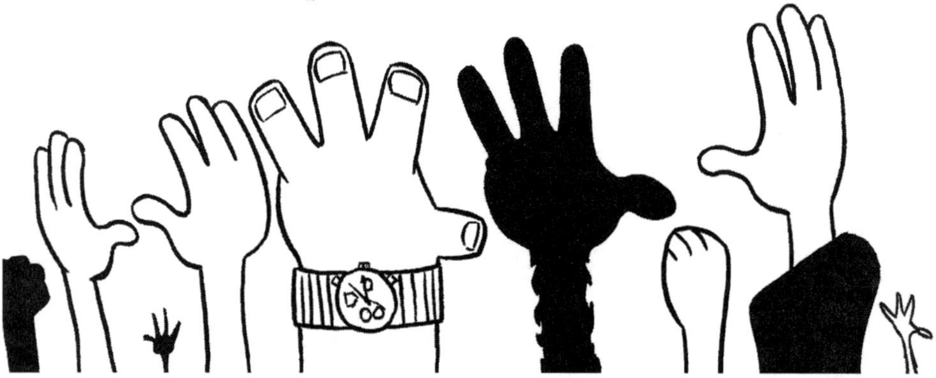

Positive aspects of this style include an increase in employee job satisfaction because they feel that their opinion matters. This ownership results in a higher quality of work because employees feel that they own their part of the equation.

A few negative aspects are that it can be a slow decision-making process because a consensus between staff and management is needed before anyone can proceed. Because of this, the company has less agility and may not address changes fast enough. And the need for a consensus can result in the best decision for the company to not be made.

What kinds of animals function with a Democratic leadership style? There are no animals that have been proven to act in a democratic way at this time. However, it is thought that some animals communicate in such a way that they are able to coordinate their actions for the good of the group. One example can be found with the humpback whale. Pods of these whales have been documented participating in a cooperative feeding behavior know as "bubble netting." Bubble netting is the action of whales blowing bubbles in a circle around a school of small fish. These bubbles act as a wall that groups the fish into a large ball that is eventually forced to the ocean's surface where the remaining whales swim up from underneath with their mouths agape catching hundreds of fish on each attempt. Somehow, a decision is made that benefits the entire group and communication is relayed that coordinates the pods efforts towards one goal.

The fourth leadership style we will look at is Laissez-Faire. In the Laissez-Faire leadership style, the employees manage their own agenda as if it were their own business. Management provides general guidelines but with minimal direction and delegates tasks as needed. Communication flows equally which is very little when compared to the other styles. This leadership style is very effective in a creative group. Often, this style occurs not from design but because of poor management. It occurs out of necessity. The downside to this leadership style can be an unfocused staff that is directionless. This can result with employees that are dissatisfied and a poor company image.

What kinds of animals function with a Laissez-Faire leadership style? Most animals operate with this style out of necessity because of poor management as well. Let's face it, they're animals. If they had the cranial capacity to be leaders who managed well, we would be living in a Planet of the Apes type world where Charleton Heston ran around in a loin cloth trying to organize the humans. But we're not and most animals operate with a Laissez-Faire leadership style. Think rabbits, deer, mosquitoes, muskrats, etc.

The fifth and final leadership style we will look at is Servant-Based. Under this style, the manager puts others, his employees, first by providing them with the resources they need to be successful. Employees under this leadership style operate with less stress, more autonomy and are more likely to become servants. This leadership style is about building a community built on trust, open communication and honest feedback to get the best out of people and unleash their true potential. The leadership style works well with passionate employees who see work as something you are and not something you do for a paycheck. Because employees work with autonomy and relationships are based on honest feedback and trust, this leadership style is at risk to employees wishing to exploit the company for their own gain. Another downside is this style works best with employees who do not need direction and it is difficult to implement in an existing structure.

The point of this exercise was to highlight the fact that leaders come in many different flavors and all have negative attributes. The trick is to either find a manager with a leadership style that you can work with, make adjustments to your working style or to become one yourself.

Lesson #3 – Who's the Boss?

How does your manager's leadership style affect you? It affects you every day. As we've seen, there are numerous leadership styles in the animal world as well as the "homo sapien" professional world. How does this knowledge affect you as an employee? By knowing there are different leadership styles out there, you can be more accommodating and understanding in dealing with a manager whose style doesn't mesh well with your working style. Maybe you work best with a Laissez-Faire style and your manager is Autocratic. Or maybe your manager works with a Democratic style and you prefer Paternalistic,. Whatever the situation, you will be able to recognize it and make adjustments to remain a productive asset to your company. As I mentioned before, there isn't a perfect leader out there. From our animal examples, in order to have a perfect leader you would have to take certain attributes from each.

If you wanted a manager who led with intelligence (chimp), curiosity (cat) and based decisions on past experiences (elephant), the perfect manager would be a chimpacatiphant. Or if you wanted a manager who led with minimal interaction (panda), quick reflexes (cat) and tireless work ethic (ant), you would want a pandacatant. And lastly, if you wanted a manager who led by being very social (elephant), a good communicator (panda) and able to carry heavy workloads (ant), you would want to be led by an elepandant.

But even this is not a true example. For every positive trait taken from each animal, a negative one would be present as well. A chimpacatiphant could have the negative traits of immaturity, aloofness and unable to cope with small details. Does that sound like any managers you've dealt with? The point is that no animal or amalgamation of animals would work just as different leadership styles would have negative traits to it as well. All managers will have positive and negative aspects to their leadership styles. It is your job as an employee to understand this and to cope with it. Managers will also adjust their styles according to the situation that they are presented with. A democratic manager may become autocratic because a deadline cannot be met if he surveyed options from employees. A Laissez-Faire manager may become Paternalistic because the team is having creative differences in finishing a project.

As you reviewed the positive, negative and managerial traits of these examples, you probably found yourself relating to a few of them. You might have recognized the domestic housecat's confidence or the ant's need for direction or the panda's territorial habits in your manager, co-workers, friends or even your family. It's a jungle out there, so be sure to watch where your step.

Tom Darrow watches Abby lie down in the shade under an oak tree signaling that she's done playing Frisbee. Tom goes back to the houseboat and gets comfortable with intentions to resume reading *Business by THE Book.* But as he begins reading he finds that their Frisbee game has worn out more than just Abby. As Tom reclines back to take a nap, he realizes that Abby got exactly what she wanted out of Tom. As Tom falls asleep he thinks that maybe Abby would be a good leader after all.

The Toonalution of ...Leading

TOONALUTION #8 - Navigating Your Way to the Next Level

Laura McBrien has never been whitewater rafting before until today. She puts on her life preserver as she listens to the instructor describe what to do if she were to fall out of the raft. She hesitates briefly as she makes a mental note to "ball up and wait" if she were to get stuck in a hydraulic boil. A hydraulic boil is later defined as a highly compressed, underwater whirlpool. This fact does not amuse her. The logic of this action makes sense as she would sink to the bottom of the river, out of the hydraulic boil and into safe waters. But her mind starts to yell, "Wouldn't you rather be watching Oprah right now!?"

Nevertheless, Laura joins the crew and they launch the raft down the Ocoee River located in the Cherokee National Forest in southeastern Tennessee. Once they make it through the first Grade IV rapid, Laura's nerves subside and she begins to enjoy herself immensely. This is a rare weekday respite from work for her. Her career has progressed rapidly over the past 24 years. It has progressed almost as rapidly as the waves and rocks which are quickly approaching her raft right now. Laura works with her crew to navigate through the rapids getting wet and thrown around in the process but remaining on the right side of dry. She smiles to herself as she realizes that her "escape" from the work week actually mirrors her pursuit of her career path. Both activities involve navigating a difficult path while overcoming and outmaneuvering obstacles in order to progress further on to the next level of responsibility and challenge.

Laura considers many of her local friends, co-workers and neighbors her family. Chief among them are her neighbors Marie and Louise, and her live-in cohabitants: her five year old Papillion dog, Beau, her housecat Sophie and her rescued cat Viggo. Laura is on the board of her neighborhood homeowner association, the Corner Oak HOA, which is a small community of townhouses in Norcross, Georgia.

Laura's personal life has always been defined by her religion. She is a practicing Christian, who went on her first mission trip a few years ago with Campus Crusade for Christ's "Care Lift/Bear Lift." They delivered food, supplies, teddy bears and the message of Jesus Christ to children in hospitals and orphanages across Russia. The Russian people had difficulty believing that complete strangers from the United States would pay thousands of dollars to serve them and their needs. Lasting twenty-four days, Laura found a love for the people and the culture of Russia and has been back on three separate missions since then.

Laura began her professional life working after high school making chocolate candy at Masters Candies in Detroit earning $2.35 an hour. Lessons learned early stayed with Laura as she received her bachelor's degree in Business Management from Oglethorpe University in Atlanta in 1990. Like most graduates taking their first uncertain steps into the business world, Laura made a few missteps going to her first interview. After sending out a "zillion" resumes to companies that had anything to do with accounting or business in general, Laura landed the interview even though it required more work experience than what she currently had. Despite the lack of experience or being one hour late because she got lost, she secured a second interview and eventually a position in the credit insurance industry.

Eventually, Laura found that her strength was in group underwriting and today she works as a Manager of Credit Union Underwriting at AEGON U.S.A. in Atlanta. She has been there for twenty-four years and is responsible for credit union credit insurance and debt protection underwriting. It is her job to make certain that the businesses AEGON invests in will be profitable and conform to company guidelines and state regulations. Her position interacts across multiple departments and services necessitating a breadth of knowledge across many functions.

Described by her coworkers as compassionate, loyal and one who leads by example, Laura has always enjoyed her work if not always the job she was in at the time. She enjoys being able to help coworkers whether it is by having the right answers, by being able to teach new employees or by acting as a sounding board for new ideas or to discuss problematic issues. Her most significant issue at work revolves around having to do more work with fewer resources. Even so, she has always been one to take a positive, proactive approach and take action and make decisions when needed.

Another wave crashes over their raft as Laura is swept back into the here and now. They have rafted their way down half of the river and everyone is having a blast. The sun is shining brightly which helps counteract the cold, fresh water that has drenched all of them numerous times. Laura recognizes that navigating through the rapids is a task easier done with the help of others. By working together, they are able to steer the raft to the next area easier without too many issues and with a smile on their faces.

Laura has many examples of being able to navigate to the next level with the help of others. One example is when she presented a proposal that would promote her to a new supervisor position. The proposal circulated to upper management but it was eventually rejected. Laura's belief that you should be patient in all situations was rewarded a few months later when the position was created and she was promoted to it.

She was successful because she navigated herself around obstacles by providing a strong proposal that was based on the needs of the company and not her own. Her manager was able to assist her by presenting it to his manager because her logic was sound and it made financial sense to the overall good of the company. Laura believes in putting your ideas out there and let them have time to flourish or fail.

Another example is when she led a mentoring group that was created to help employees identify and pursue their desired career path. Laura supported classes such as resume writing, preparing for a performance review, and completing internal job applications. Employees would go from department to department and talk with the employees about what they did, what skill sets were needed and what were the next steps to pursue working in that department. Both employees and managers saw the event as a great success. While this effort did not result in a promotion for Laura, it is an example of how she was able to navigate to another level of responsibility. This experience will provide other benefits to her career going forward including the addition of skill sets, managing direct reports and networking across business functions to her resume.

Laura believes that, as an employee, you have to take responsibility for promoting yourself. She realizes that managers are busy with their own jobs and promoting their own career development. One way that Laura promotes herself is by keeping a list of all of her job tasks. Each time a performance review comes due, she compares the new list to the old and makes note of all the new tasks she's taken on since the last review. She notes what projects she's completed, what teams she has participated on and what her contributions were including any training and/or education she's completed. While using this method does not ensure a promotion, it has helped Laura secure larger raises every year than before she kept such records.

Throughout these experiences, Laura realized something vital to her career path. She realized that she wants to be a "producer" of work that impacts her company's profitability and not a "reporter" of other people's work. This realization is critical as Laura identifies which path, or river, her career will progress to next and what obstacles she will have to overcome going forward.

The Toonalution of Laura McBrien

Like whitewater rafting, navigating your way to the next level has many challenges. You must have a destination in mind. You will encounter many obstacles along the way. Some will set you back, while others will change the path you are on; and, if you are not careful, some will stop your progression totally.

Do you want to progress upward in your company to a position of more responsibility and scope? If so, why? Is it for professional growth? Do you want to get promoted because it is the next stepping stone on your career path? That is, it provides you with the experience and training you need to stay on course to your desired end position? Or is it because you feel it would be a position that incorporates all of your strengths and would be your "dream job"?

Or do you want to get promoted for personal gain? Personal gain could be defined as having a higher salary, better benefits or a more flexible schedule. Or is it for both professional gain and personal gain? Whatever the reason, take ownership of your career path and start your journey by taking the first step. In this example, that first step is into a whitewater raft.

Unless an employee chooses to remain in a particular position for his entire career, he or she typically wants to progress within the organization to higher levels of responsibility. This upward path involves skill, planning, support and even a little luck for success to happen. Even with these factors working for them, they cannot remain silent and hope that it all works out for the best. A proactive approach will benefit the employee greatly if done in the correct manner. In this chapter, we will explore how an employee remains successful in his current role while preparing for his next role by comparing it to rafting down a whitewater river. Both scenarios include seven steps:

1. Get a Guide
2. Identify Your Destination
3. Don't Get Wet
4. Get Into It!
5. Stroke! Stroke! Stroke!
6. Leverage Your Crew
7. Ride the Bull!
8. Get Back on the Bus

Once you have decided that you do want to progress upward in your company, what is your next step? What is your plan going forward? Is it one that will give you the experience and exposure you need to the right, decision-making people? Or are you hoping that by working hard you will be noticed and promoted? In most cases, hard work is never enough. Why not? Because everyone works hard: especially those who hope to be promoted. You have to differentiate yourself from what I call the "Hard Working Herd." How do you do that? More importantly, what is your first step?

Step #1 - Get a Guide

For whitewater rafting, getting a guide is paramount for safety concerns. Without a guide, you increase your risk for bodily injury because you do not know where the obstacles will be, but you also do not know how to maneuver around them. You could try it on your own and possibly succeed. But it will be a rougher, longer ride where the obstacles hit you head-on. Without a guide, you increase the chances you will not finish to the end.

Before you embark upon whitewater rafting, the guide always takes a few moments to go over the basic strokes. Once everyone has the basic stokes down, the guide will have everyone practice the basic maneuvers to make sure everyone is able to navigate down the river appropriately. The faster everyone is able to grasp the maneuvers, the faster the guide is able to start the journey.

If the guide feels everyone has a strong handle on what he is asking everyone to do, he will feel more assured to take the passengers on a more adventurous path down the river. Similarly, if you grasp your new position quickly, your manager might do the same for you. By putting you on a more adventurous and challenging path, success on your part will lead to a quicker path to the next promotion.

For your career, the first step is to find a mentor to be your guide. This step will take some investigating on your part. A mentor will help you plan your long-term career development and identify challenges you will face going forward. If your company offers a mentoring program, ask to be a part of it. But, getting a mentor does not have to be through a sponsored program. If there is a manager you have a positive relationship with who is not your direct manager, reach out to them. If they are not open to being your mentor, chances are they will offer some additional contacts who might work out even better.

Another way to find a mentor is to ask an employee in the department you really want to work in to go to lunch with you. Ask them what it will take to get a job in their area. Subscribe to trade journals and/or join a trade association in the field you're interested in. This will also help you begin to build a network (your whitewater rafting crew) which we will talk about momentarily.

Remember, your career path will span over thirty years of service. Do not be in a hurry. If you are, you may sacrifice a short-term win for a long-term set back. Everyone has heard the phrase "Don't burn bridges." Put another way, keep all paths open. The co-worker you can't wait to get away from in your current position may be your manager in a future position. This doesn't mean you have to be friends with everyone you work with. You just need to maintain a professional relationship with them.

Step #2 - Identify Your Destination

For rafting, knowing where to go is as easy as referencing a map of the river or by hiring a guide to help you navigate safely. These maps show not only the direction of the currents but also potential obstacles. This is where having a mentor at work can help you greatly. They will have the experience and expertise to help you identify possible obstacles and come up with solutions to overcome them.

For your career, identifying your destination is to identify what your end position is. To help do this, you need help from your mentor. If you are unable to participate in a mentoring program that offers insight into other departments within a company, ask to work with someone in a field you find interesting on your day off. You owe it to yourself and the company to make a due diligence effort to identify a career path you will find rewarding and challenging. This position could be a goal you wish to attain in five, ten or more years depending on where you are on your career path. If you are fresh out of college, be aggressive! Challenge yourself by setting a goal that is both aggressive and inspirational.

Once you have figured out your dream job, the path to get there becomes clearer. If you cannot identify your dream job, that's ok. You may not feel comfortable saying you want to be the next Regional Vice President because you do not understand all the aspects of the position or the demands involved. But you may find that you are comfortable identifying a role a few levels below that role as a destination. Whatever the situation, you can now identify the positions and experiences needed to get the role you desire. These are steps in your career path.

Do you want to do your manager's job? When you consider this, include all facets of his or her job. Do not factor only the positive aspects of it. Just because his company car is nicer and he has stock options doesn't mean that is the job for you. If you do not know all of the facets of his job, ask him. Also ask him if he could see you in his position at some point. If he cannot see you in his position, ask why not. It may be that you are lacking some basic credentials for the position or you need additional experience which you can get by progressing to other positions within the company. Be mindful of his advice. This type of advice, what skill sets you need, positions to achieve, will clarify further the steps in your career path.

Look at other companies to see what type of positions they offer. If you have certain passions in life, a hobby for example, see if there is a way to combine your work life with one of your personal passions. If you are able to do this, you will enjoy your job greatly and be very successful at it. This book is an example of this. I enjoy working in the business world, but I also have a creative side that I express through writing and illustrating. By writing this book, I am able to combine all three as well as my love of public speaking. Don't let someone else's rules contain your dream!

Step #3 - Don't Get Wet

For rafting, this step is self-explanatory. Just don't get wet! Either when you get into the raft or while you are waiting for directions from your guide. Get a secure footing in the raft and solicit help from your crew to help you in. Once in, do what you have to get in a secure seated position. On most rafts, you do this by sliding one foot up underneath the thwart, or inflatable bench, in front and your heel under the one behind you.

For work, you do not "get wet" by continuing to do a great job in your current position. This should be an easy step for you to accomplish because you should not pursue a promotion until you have proven yourself in your current role. Why is this step necessary? It is necessary because no one will recommend you for higher levels of responsibility if you cannot handle your current workload. Every factor counts here from your ability to complete mundane tasks to heading up special projects. Many more eyes and opinions on how you are doing will follow you as you pursue a promotion. You cannot falter in any respect because one small failure may become an unsurpassable obstacle blocking your career path.

If you feel you are ready for a promotion, but no one else does, you need to raise your game. The best way to do this is to get a peer mentor. This is someone who is either fulfilling the position you are in or has done it recently in the past. A peer mentor will help you accelerate your performance immediately if picked correctly. You want a peer mentor who is setting the high performance standard in your department. This person is probably considered a High-Potential (Hi-Po) employee who is on the career fast track. The Hi-Po employee will keep you challenged, be on the front edge of any new projects or learning paths and will be a great networking connection as your career progresses. If you are unsure as to whom this is in your department, ask yourself, whose performance intimidates you? You are intimidated for a reason, find out what it is and why. What are they doing that you are not? What best practices can you incorporate into your working day? This relationship will breed competition between the two of you, increasing the performance level of both.

Step #4 - Get Into It

For rafting this would be to challenge yourself to become involved with your crew to row the best you can. Listen to your guide, follow his directions and pull your weight in effort. If you have been rafting before, get more involved by sitting in front where you hit the rapids first. Go after the waves with enthusiasm and purpose. Don't relegate yourself to being the uninvolved crewman who has a white-knuckled death grip on the paddle and doesn't participate. Encourage your crewmates by celebrating the successful navigation of a rapid and the comradely of a job well done.

For work, the fourth step is to take on additional responsibility that will give you the experience you will need in your future position. For example, if you work in a clothing store and want to move into management, ask you manager what tasks they do that you could help them accomplish. Just by taking the initiative to ask the question will put you ahead of your peers. While your manager might not be able to do exactly what you asked, they will probably offer up some other tasks that you could help them with. Whatever they assign to you, do it to your best ability! Successfully finishing these tasks correctly is what will encourage them to give you more responsibility.

If this is not possible, schedule "work with" training days with people in the position you would like to achieve one day. Go through your manager to schedule as they should be your first point of contact. You do not want to be seen as someone who goes outside the chain of command. If your manager is not supportive, go to his/her manager but do it in a tactful way. Do not speak negatively of your manager. Instead approach it as a developmental opportunity that will make you a more productive employee and allow you to explore options for your career path. Be sure to take periodical temperature checks and ask yourself, do you have the drive and determination to go the distance?

Step #5 - Stroke! Stroke! Stroke!

As you navigate down the rapids you will find out two things very quickly: which strokes work for you and which ones work against you. Once you find this out, pick your best stroke and go with it. Encourage your crew to remain in synch with each other and to respond quickly to the commands from the guide. By doing this, you and the crew will navigate the rapids in a more efficient and effective manner, maximizing the enjoyment of the journey. You will be a valuable asset to the guide and the crew.

For your career, you need to compile a list of best practices you want to enact on your first day in your new position. These are ideas and strategies that you have seen implemented successfully by employees in the role you desire. This step works in conjunction with the previous step. As you take on additional responsibility, reach out to others to see what works the best for them. If you work with ten different people, you will find at least ten new best practices.

When you do reach the role you desire, implement as many best practices as you can immediately. Even if only three or four come to fruition, those will be three or four more than you had before. The six or seven that fail will not be remembered as failures. You will be applauded, and remembered, for your effort in trying something new and challenging the status quo of the role.

These best practices do not have to be perfect but they need to show a strong grasp of what the job responsibilities are and are meant to "raise the bar" on the current standard. No one will fault you for trying something new. Those that do, do so from a position of weakness. They are threatened by your attempt to raise the standard of performance. A standard they are used to and probably not willing to leave. You want your new coworkers to feel uncomfortable in operating in their comfort zone.

One of the most accepted ways to get a head start in a new position is to construct a plan based on a set timeframe. The most common is a 100-day plan. Rather than getting into specifics here, it has been mentioned as a resource to look up. Most 100-day plans are created to show that you, during the initial interview, took the time and did the research to not only create one but to also understand the position more. It will help separate you from the other interview candidates. Since you do not always know all the aspects of the job you are interviewing for, complete accuracy is not necessary.

Step #6 - Leverage Your Crew

The further you progress down the river, the more in synch your crew becomes to each other. This is the first step to becoming a high performance whitewater rafting machine. You will be able to rely on your crew to help you face new challenges and enhance your journey. They will be able to rely on you for the same level of protection and support. You might not ever need their help, but you will be thankful for it when you do.

For work, the sixth step is to leverage your network, your crew, to pursue open positions that are on your career path. This network will encompass most of the people you interact with professionally. This would include your mentor, coworkers, superiors or acquaintances outside your company who work in your industry.

Your network is something that must be nurtured over time. Build relationships with your coworkers and try not to burn any bridges during your career. You never know what path your career or your coworkers' careers will go. You may end up working with them, or for them one day. By having a network of individuals both at your company, and through networking groups in your city, you will be in touch with not only the open positions in your industry, but also emerging trends and a source for job leads if needed.

Step #7 - Ride the Bull!

As you become more adept as a whitewater rafter, you may find the ride lacking the challenge you need to keep your interest or desire to stay on course. This is the moment when discouragement and boredom may rear their ugly heads. Do not become complacent in your role. Becoming complacent will open you, and your crew, up to new dangers that will threaten, and possibly upset your journey.

To offset this, you and your crew could play games, sing songs or challenge yourselves to raise your performance level. You could raise your performance level by directing the guide to steer the raft down a rougher path, thereby taking on bigger rapids. Another way is for you to "Ride the Bull." Riding the Bull is when a rafter climbs on the bow of the raft with their legs hanging over the edge. They hold onto the lead rope and go feet first into the next rapid. As the rider, you are not steering the raft, but you are having a great time. Rough, wet and prohibited by many insurance companies, it is a guaranteed way to keep the excitement going when the ride gets stale. And it will help reinvigorate you and your crew to complete your journey.

For work, you would want to "Ride the Bull" to help you to not get discouraged and to stay on task as you pursue a promotion. There are many reasons you could get discouraged. You may not have been asked to interview for a position you desire. You may have interviewed but did not get the position or positive feedback. You may have interviewed but the decision has been delayed because of budget concerns.

Not getting discouraged is a task that is easier said in theory than done in real world situations. But it is very important to remember that the way you handle rejection will be observed by the people who interviewed you. If you do not handle it well, you will probably not be interviewed for that position again.

"Handling it well" does not mean you have to smile and agree with the feedback, if any, provided. It does mean that you should respond in a proactive, constructive way that shows you understand the concerns management has with placing you in the desired position. With this understanding, you will be able to address the issue, taking it off the table during the next interview. This will show that you are mature enough to own your career path, intelligent enough to act on constructive criticism and adept enough to learn new skill sets needed for the position. Never shy away from constructive criticism.

An example of this is when a colleague of mine interviewed three different times over eighteen months for a District Manager position she felt she deserved. Because she handled herself well after being passed over, she was given another opportunity. Not only should you handle yourself graciously in this situation, you should take it as an opportunity to find out what you need to work on to be ready for the next interview. In her case, she needed to work on her "Team Development" skills. So she worked on turning her weakness, her developmental opportunity, that was identified as constructive criticism in one interview into a strength for the next interview.

Also, you never know how some situations might result. Because she wasn't promoted until the third opening, she ended up taking over the sales team she was on five years earlier. She did not have to move, which she would have had to do for the other two positions, and she was in a very high profile area which gave her access to a larger network of decision-makers. Because of this, she was able to build relationships across many departments and functions which increased the size of her network.

Learn from the negative situations you experience and be mindful that, once you have your first interview, you are on a timetable. If you do not secure a job within the first two or three interviews, you will probably be pulled off the promotable list for a while. This will be a very difficult list to get your name back on so do not relent in addressing your opportunities.

Be selective in the positions you pursue and keep them in synch with your career path. If you push really hard for a promotion, and then you turn it down for some reason such as location, you will hurt your credibility and might not be asked to interview again.

Step #8 – Get Back on the Bus

Finally, when you've safely left the rapids and returned to terra firma, don't check the experience off as being done never to do again. Begin planning your next adventure and raise the stakes by challenging yourself to a more difficult river. This means getting back on the bus. Most rafting companies transport passengers in old school buses that have been painted in wild colors with the rafts stacked and strapped down on top. The ride is initially rough, smelly and uncomfortable. But once you are on your way, you will begin planning ways to improve your performance to tackle this new, exciting challenge.

For work, your first few weeks in your new position might not be rough but they will be hectic. Whatever you do, do not take a relaxed attitude to owning your new role. The first three months are the most important months in any job. It is within this timeframe that you will make your first impression on your manager, co-workers and customers. What you do in this timeframe will represent you as other people speak of you. It is very important that you work hard to not only learn your new position quickly, but to show an understanding of not only what your job is, but how it is affected and affects other positions within the company. Building new relationships, understanding your manager's expectations, performing the role, implementing your 100-day plan: you will have more than enough to keep you busy for a while so it is important that you stay organized and on task.

Execute your 60, 90 or 100 day plan and show results immediately. Nothing will show your new manager that he or she made the right decision in selecting than your showing measurable results immediately. In doing this, your new coworkers will see you as an equal and hopefully as a competitor. Take this as a compliment. If they see you as a competitor, meaning you have pushed them out of their comfort zone, you are doing something they either haven't thought of, or something that they have not been able to do in the past.

Suggestion – take one project or task and follow it through to completion. If you do this, you will be known as someone who can get the job done right the first time. Challenge yourself but be careful to not over commit yourself to a task beyond your abilities.

Once you begin to get comfortable in your role, you need to "Get Back on the Bus!" You'll need to assess where you are on your career path. What is your next step? What role or experience do you need to progress further "down the river" towards you final destination? Keep yourself challenged and you will continue to grow professionally and personally. And you will raise your own performance standards and those of others around you as well. If enough employees "Get Back on the Bus," the entire company will benefit from an increase in employee performance and morale.

You are probably asking yourself, what would happen if you were to do nothing? What would happen if you stayed in the same position you are in currently? What would happen if you do not increase your productivity or contribute to the company's success in another positive way? What if you never went whitewater rafting?

The most positive scenario that could occur is that nothing would happen. You would remain in the same position, on the same calm lake, that you were on before. You would remain "safe" from the rewards of a new challenge. You might remain safe in your position until you retire. But that scenario is less and less likely to occur in these tough economic times. And remember, if you do not test yourself, if you do not continuously learn new skills, those that you have will become stale from disuse. Just like the whitewater paddle that becomes brittle from lack of use, your value as an asset to the company may become brittle as well. While a proactive stance executed with a cohesive plan will attain results in most cases, failure in attaining success still places you in a better position than you were in previously.

You may also be asking yourself, what would happen to your career path if you let your hard work speak for itself as merit for promotion? Hard workers have been promoted and will continue to be promoted in the future. But when this happens, there probably are some other factors to go along with it. It might happen because of the ease of placement. Maybe you are a qualified candidate who does not have to be relocated to a different site. Whatever these factors are, don't rely on circumstances to be the driving force of your career. You should be the driving force of your career. Take ownership.

It is your right as an employee to just do your job as it was described to you at your hiring and hope that hard work will lead to a promotion. But by not pursuing a promotion actively, your manager may not have confidence in your ability to handle more responsibility. He might wonder if you would you be as inactive in the new role as you are in your current role? Why would he want to put his name on the line if you are unwilling to do the same? So, what can you do today? Grab your paddle and jump in the raft!

Laura lifts her paddle as they reach the end of their journey downriver. Wet, cold and tired, Laura looks back at the river that brought them here and marvels at what a great time they had despite the risks involved. She knows the trek would have been much more difficult and not as much fun if she had done it alone. Through careful navigation around the obstacles that came their way, they were able to remain on course continuing their journey.

Laura realizes that she could have stayed home and watched Oprah in her living room with Beau, Sophie and Viggo. But she would have missed an adventure that challenged her both physically and mentally. And just like navigating your way down a whitewater river, navigating your career path is less daunting and more rewarding if done with a plan, with direction from a guide and with the help of others.

Laura makes a pact with herself to pursue the next steps in her career path by reaching out to those coworkers in the position she hopes to occupy one day. She plans on asking them to be her mentor and help her navigate around the obstacles before her. As she puts her paddle, life vest and helmet in the bus for the ride back, she decides she will go whitewater rafting again and soon. Maybe she will invite her neighbors or a coworker. Or maybe she will invite the manager she hopes will be her mentor soon. Or maybe, she'll bring Beau.

The Toonalution of ...Career Ambition

TOONALUTION #9 - Playing the Expectations Game

Harriett Frankel pauses outside of a local video game store on her way to the grocers. She stops because she is drawn to a video game display in which two neighborhood boys are engrossed in competition. They are white-knuckling the controllers in a vain attempt to outplay each other to victory. Harriett doesn't know what type of game they're playing, only that it looks much too involved for her tastes. Both boys are hitting a series of buttons in seemingly random order while man-handling two small joysticks. Harriett can't help but to laugh as she thinks how shocking it would be to them if she were to join their game. No one would ever expect a woman of her age being able to do such a thing. She continues on to the grocery store anxious to see how her "For Rent" advertisement turned out in the neighborhood flyer.

Surpassing expectations is something Harriett Frankel has been doing for over ninety years now. Born on October 29, 1916 in Cook County Hospital in Chicago, Illinois, Harriett's early childhood and young adult life were defined by the economic hardships of the Great Depression.

Along the way to celebrating her ninety-fourth birthday in 2010, Harriett overcame decades of personal challenges placed on her by others. One of the first ones was for being Jewish during a time of religious intolerance during and after World War II. Another was for being a woman in the male-dominated working environment of the 1950s and 1960s.

Harriett faced religious intolerance with a very head-on approach: she didn't stand for it. While working at an ad agency, she was approached by a Klu Klux Klan member whose local chapter was a tenant in the same office building. He made it a point to tell her that he knew she was a Jew, but that she had nothing to fear from him. While the threat was veiled, her reaction was not. She decided that she was not going to work in an environment of racial prejudice no matter how accommodating the Klan pretended to be. She quit working there shortly after that event and secured another position as a commercial artist at Eastburn Siegel Advertising. While there she designed brochures for the local black dentists and met her future husband, Norman, who worked as a copywriter. Shortly after their meeting, he proposed to her while on horseback and they remained married for 53 years until his death at the age of 84.

Sexism manifested itself in many ways. Even though she had the financial means to secure a loan for her first business, an all-girl advertising agency, the bank forced her husband to co-sign it to vouch for her financial stability. Even more insulting, she had to have him cosign another, much smaller loan, to buy a point-and-shoot camera. Sexism was seen at her workplace as well. The local union would not allow her to join, stating it was an organization for "Men Only."

Harriett attended Georgia School of Technology in 1941 before women were allowed to enroll and before its name was changed in 1948 to Georgia Institute of Technology. Women were not admitted until the Board of Regents of the State of Georgia voted in 1952. Harriett did this through a program implemented during World War II to support the troops. She worked in the engineering department reading blueprints to help build B29 bombers which were eventually used to drop the atomic bomb on Hiroshima, Japan, on August 6, 1945 beginning the end of World War II.

Harriett worked at the Bell Bomber Plant in Marietta, Georgia, and attended free drafting courses while commuting eighty miles roundtrip until she became pregnant with the first of her three children. When Lockheed Corporation, later Lockheed Martin, replaced Bell after the war, Harriett was told that she had to re-interview for her position. When she did, she was told that they did not need women anymore since the war was over. Eventually they came back and asked her to work for them. Her response was short and to the point; she told them to "shove it!"

Harriett exceeded expectations by not conforming to the confining roles society placed on her. Not only was she able to move herself into a better place from a career perspective, she was also able to rewrite the rules of business by becoming a successful business woman and entrepreneur.

One of the more significant obstacles Harriet has overcome is the loss of her hearing. Her mother discovered this when she was a small child. The loss was gradual until she had to get her first hearing aid when she was in her early twenties. Eventually, Harriett's hearing deteriorated further to where even the strongest hearing aid was ineffective. She endured many operations and, as technology improved, she received a cochlear implant. Unfortunately, the deterioration continued to where she eventually became totally deaf. Even so, Harriett has kept a positive perspective on her situation. She is known to say, "being deaf is easier than getting old!"

Harriett's mother was from Louisville, Kentucky, and her father was from Kiev, Ukraine, Russia. He worked as a traveling salesman who peddled silk and satin to the local funeral homes and brothels, selling purported eternal comfort to one and earthly desires to the other. Harriett credits her parent's diverse upbringings as influencing her desire to travel. She has visited twelve countries around the world including Cuba before Fidel Castro came to power and Sweden to celebrate her ninetieth birthday.

At times opinionated and blunt, Harriett started her own ad agency and moved to the center of Atlanta because it was convenient for her customers. She retired as the Art Director of her own ad agency when she became totally deaf and larger agencies with TV and radio expertise became more prevalent.

Like the neighborhood boys in the arcade, playing games has always been a big part of Harriett's life. Growing up, she would describe herself as a tomboy. Back then, the games she played included tag, kick-the-can, jump rope and baseball with the boys where she once broke her finger trying to make a game-saving play. As an adult, her hobbies have included tennis, golf and riding horseback. She learned to rollerblade when she was sixty and lately Harriett has enjoyed playing bridge and exercising at the local Baptist church. She enjoys the theater and ballet and writes articles for the 2 Hard of Hearing/Deaf group. Recently she was asked to write a monthly column for the ALDA Reader (Association of Late-Deafened Adults) which supports the empowerment of late-deafened people.

Once she arrives at the grocery store, Harriett reviews the advertisement she placed in the neighborhood flyer. She rents out two apartments in a local house she owns. Satisfied with the results, she heads home and passes by the two boys who are still battling for video game supremacy. She thinks back to the games she's played in the past including bridge. Unlike playing a video game, she feels comfortable with the rules of bridge, the strategies needed to win, the obstacles she may face and the pursuit of winning. She smiles realizing that the way she plays bridge is very similar to the way she overcame expectations in the working world. With both, she learned the rules, understood the tools, identified obstacles and pursued a reward. She sees now that she was very good at "Playing the Expectations Game."

This is knowledge she would love to share with the boys, but their attention would be hard to break at this time. She reckons that today's teenagers would be more likely to relate her thoughts of "Playing the Expectations Game" to playing a video game rather than to a game of bridge.

The Toonalution of Harriett Frankel

Everyone has certain expectations of other people. A customer in a restaurant has an expectation of service from his waiter or waitress. A passenger in a taxi has an expectation of arriving at her destination in a timely manner. A football player has an expectation of direction, training and leadership from his coach. A constituent has certain expectations from her politician. It is how adept someone anticipates and addresses expectations that determine how successful they will be in attaining their desired reward. This is called "Playing the Expectations Game."

It is the waiter or the taxi cab driver who exceeds the customer's expectations who will receive a larger tip. It is the football player who exceeds his coach's expectations who will play as a starter. It is the constituent whose expectations are met or surpassed who will vote for the same politician again and again. It is the person who plays the Expectations Game and wins who receives the desired reward.

Are you playing the Expectations Game as an employee at work? Do you know the rules of the game and how it's played? Do you know what tools are available to you and what obstacles you might encounter and how to overcome them? Do you know the rewards that you are playing for?

In this chapter, we will discuss how an employee should interact with his manager to produce a relationship built around trust, honesty and a desire to accomplish common goals by comparing "Playing the Expectations Game" to playing a video game.

Video games have transformed from the square blocks of Space Invaders in 1978 into the virtual reality of Mass Effect 2 released in 2010. They have transformed beyond the world of teenage entertainment into practical applications that are utilized across diverse industries. Leap Frog utilizes video games to teach children everything from basic colors for a six month old to Algebra for a fourteen year old. Medical institutions and historical organizations are using video "games" to assist in surgery and in recreating historical wars of our past. The video game Rockstar is the first video game in which you can learn how to play a musical instrument.

How is playing video games similar to playing the Expectations Game? Simple, for both games you must know what are the goals, rules, tools, obstacles and rewards. How you perform in both situations determines whether you succeed or not in completing the tasks given to you.

For example, in the video game, Super Mario Galaxy, your overall goal is to save Princess Peach from Bowser, the evil snapping turtle. To do this, Mario retrieves "Power Stars" that have been scattered across different galaxies by completing quests or defeating enemies. Secondary goals include defeating the evil henchmen of Bowser, collecting Star Bits, Goal Coins and finding hidden treasures. These secondary goals do not need to be completed but they will greatly assist in achieving the primary goal to save Princess Peach. The player will inadvertently complete some of them just through pursuing the primary goal, but it is not necessary. However, if the player does pursue these secondary goals, they will have more support, energy and player lives in which to pursue their primary goal.

Playing the Expectations Game is "played" the same way. Every employee has a primary goal of their job. While you are working to achieve this goal, you should identify secondary goals as they relate to your relationship with your manager. By figuring out what your manager's expectations are of you beyond the primary goal, you will begin building trust (support), find motivation to do a good job (energy) and increase your opportunities (player lives) for career advancement. In order to play the "Expectations Game", you must understand the seven success factors. They are:

1. Which Game to Play....
2. Got Change?
3. Rescue, Defeat or Solve?
4. I Wouldn't Touch That
5. Fire, Jump, Throw, Duck & Weave
6. Ouch! What Was That?
7. Gold Coins and Power Stars!

We will compare these factors between the "Super Mario Galaxy" video game to a real life example an employee might experience at work.

Factor #1 – Which Game to Play...

For our video game example you have to pick which game you want to play. The best choice is always one that compliments your current skill sets. If you're a good shot with a rifle, then a shoot-them-up game would be ideal. If you are athletic, a sports game would make sense because you would already know the rules and goals of the game. If you pick a game you are not familiar with, it will involve a bigger investment in both time and money to become competitive.

For playing the Expectations Game the first step is to identify whose game you want to play. Ask yourself, whose expectations do you need to perform against to achieve your desired reward? As an employee, you have many important relationships to maintain. This could be with your manager, your peers or with a division within the company such as marketing, customer service or sales. Whoever they are, those relationships are important because they help you get your job done in an effective and efficient way.

But the most important relationship you have at work should be the one you have with your immediate supervisor. It is his or her expectations you need to perform against to achieve your goals and realize your rewards. Why? Because your manager is the one person who knows what you are supposed to be doing, when you are supposed to be doing it and how you are doing against the goals outlined for you. She knows what you desire from your position and where you would like for your career to progress to. She needs to understand what you want out of them just as much as you need to know what she wants out of you. By understanding your manager's expectations of you, your path to realizing your goals will become clearly defined and easier to accomplish.

Your manager is the eyes and ears of upper management, human resources and other divisions that you may want to work for in the future as your career progresses. Do not provide your manager with the bricks to block your career path. Do not let her create your story. Create your own story by exceeding the expectations of you and your role.

What about you, the employee, who may not have much interaction with your manager on a regular basis? The same statement applies except it will be based upon fewer interactions which makes each interaction that much more important. One bad interaction could translate into a week's worth of bad decisions if you do not manage expectations carefully.

You may be someone who performs to your job description and feels that you do not have to play the Expectations Game. This would be a false assumption. The expectations that your manager has of you go beyond the goals of your job description. These expectations are not only of your performance and ability to complete your job effectively, but also of how well you react in different situations.

Most managers do not sit an employee down and say, "This is what you are going to do, this is how you're going to do it, here is a list of my expectations of you in this role and all unsaid expectations as well." Often, the employee is left to their own devices to figure out how best to perform a task and the rules are figured out by trial-and-error.

What expectations does your manager have of you? What are your performance expectations? What are your communication expectations? If you do not know what her expectations are, you need to ask her to clarify. Why? Because without a strong sense of what is expected of you, you will not know how you are progressing against those expectations. You should expect and request annual reviews of your performance expectations against actual results. You will never know where you need to improve if you do not know where you stand. By making this request, it forces your manager to communicate her expectations to you and it holds her accountable against them as well.

Think about how you interact with your manager. What do you do? What do you not do? Do you react quickly, without much thought? Or do you react in a more measured way that reflects your thought process? Do you have the same sense of urgency to her goals that you have to your own? What are some common results of your actions? Is your ability to achieve your goals helped or hampered by your responses? Do you respond with only your needs represented or do you think of others' needs as well?

Most jobs involve more than what is described in the job description or what was initially communicated to you by your manager or human resource representative. The key is to find out what is most important to your manager and address those goals first. This will score immediate points and you will be known as someone who can get things accomplished. After you've completed a string of these, you will be seen as the go-to-person in the office which may cause jealousy with your co-workers. That is fine. Their issue is not with you and the job you are doing, even though it will seem like it. Their issue is with their inability to keep pace with your results. They will feel challenged even though you may have never spoken to them directly. Be prepared for it and relish in it. Be concerned when they do not feel challenged because that means that you're performance level has declined and they no longer see you as a threat.

From your manager's perspective, her expectations are the rules of the game. If you break one of these rules, you will be punished in some way for it. It may be in a minor way such as a disapproving look or comment. Or it may be in a more serious way such as putting you on a performance improvement plan, by not supporting your desire to be promoted or in the extreme circumstances, termination.

Factor #2 – Got Change?

In order to play a video game in an arcade, you have to pay for it. For most arcades found in casual dining restaurants or shopping malls the cost is fifty cents to one dollar per game. If you're lucky, you may find a Pac-Man or Joust tabletop game circa 1983 for twenty-five cents. For the arcades that are a small part of a larger entertainment establishment, you have to place money on a gaming card and games cost anywhere from two to ten dollars for interactive games. In order to play the game, you have to be willing to invest your time and resources in pursuit of a thrilling experience.

As an employee playing the Expectations Game, you must be willing to invest your resources as well. Your resources are your time, knowledge, skills and monetary resources. An investment in time might manifest itself by staying late to finish a project ahead of its deadline. An investment in knowledge and/or skill could be from taking additional training classes or by working beyond the scope of your job description to add value to your team. And an investment of monetary resources could be from taking those additional training classes or educational classes in pursuit of a college degree or MBA.

Before you begin, take time to understand the potential costs to you. How do you do that? Ask yourself if you are willing to spend extra time, brain power, expertise and money to play the game. Without this understanding, you may run out of drive prior to finishing the Expectations Game.

Factor #3 – Rescue, Defeat or Solve?

In a video game, you must identify the goal so you understand in which direction you need to go. For example, are you supposed to rescue someone, defeat an enemy or solve a mystery? The goal will vary depending on what type of game is played. For a sports game the goal is typically to defeat an opponent which could be an individual or team. For a first-person shooter game, the goal is to battle evil forces. For classic video games such as Pac-Man, Space Invaders and Pong, the goals were very simple: to eat dots, to shoot aliens and to hit the ball. Whatever the goal, understand it and pursue it to the best of your abilities.

For our example in Super Mario Galaxy, the primary goal is to vanquish the evil Bowser and rescue Princess Peach from his fortress. This is done by collecting "Power Stars" to open new galaxies and defeating numerous "Bosses" which will eventually lead to the hidden fortress.

Secondary goals include vanquishing evil henchmen, navigating through hazardous worlds and collecting bonus stars.

For the Expectations Game, your primary goal is to vanquish your own "Bad Guy." As an employee, your "Bad Guy" is the challenge of being able to perform your job functions to a high level while addressing your manager's expectations quickly. Like most "Bad Guys," this challenge looks very intimidating at first, but, once you identify the real challenge, it is not. Your manager's biggest expectations will most likely be in line with your job description so concentrate on learning and performing your job very well. If you are not new to your position, revisit your job description and ask your manager where he sees room for improvement.

Secondary goals include overcoming daily obstacles, building relationships with your coworkers and customers, navigating your way through office politics and achieving smaller wins in pursuit of your primary goal.

Factor #4 – I Wouldn't Touch That

In a video game, understanding why things happen the way they do is to understand the rules of the game. In Indiana Jones and the Temple of Doom, Indy famously tells his sidekick, Shorty to "Step where I step and don't touch anything." Shorty proceeds to touch a lamp triggering a trap door from which two mummies fall out. Because Shorty did not follow the rules, he placed himself and Indiana Jones in jeopardy. While this makes for great entertainment on the silver screen, it would feel like a bad B-movie if it happened to you.

There are three major rules for our video game example, Mario's Super Galaxy:

1. Do not venture into harm's way
2. Do not come into contact with harmful forces
3. Do not get hit by an enemy's attack

This sounds easy doesn't it? But not when you begin playing the game and realize these harmful entities are found around, and sometimes on, the path you must take. They manifest themselves as bottomless pits, raging waterfalls, hostile creatures and walls of fire. Sometimes, you inadvertently venture into harm's way simply because you are not familiar with the environment. Other times, you are forced to come into contact with harmful forces because they are blocking your path to success. And lastly, at times, enemies will appear that will attack you. They will attempt to stop your progress by taking aggressive action against you. In order to continue playing, you must navigate your way through harm's way, around harmful forces to continue towards your goal.

For the Expectations Game these same rules apply. As an employee, you may inadvertently venture into harm's way because you are not familiar with your new office environment. An example of this is dealing with office politics. Without knowing the politics present in an office, you could say the wrong thing to the wrong person or support an idea your manager campaigned against. There are many situations that may place you in harm's way just from a lack of knowledge.

Your path may become blocked by harmful forces. A harmful force could be a subordinate who resists your direction because he doesn't want to be challenged to raise his own performance level. Or your path could be blocked by your own lack of knowledge. Maybe you are not familiar with the computer operating system used or the processes in place to perform your job skills.

Also enemies may appear that will attempt to stop your progress by taking aggressive action against you. An enemy could be the employee in the cube next to you who downplays your work ethic to coworkers because he is threatened by your results. Or it could be a manager who muddies the communication path because his agenda is different from that of your manager.

But unlike a video game, there are a few unwritten rules that must be understood in order to succeed at the Expectations Game:

1. Address urgent requests urgently – Make what is urgent to your manager urgent to you. This will build trust and you will be seen as the go-to employee. Don't know what's urgent to your manager? Ask!
2. Prepare for more – At the point where most managers feel an employee has "gotten" their new job, she will ask more from them. You may feel you are not competent enough in your new job to take on additional responsibility, so you must learn it quickly so you are prepared for the added challenge when it is asked of you.
3. Do not let your manager feel foolish – You are only as good as your manager's opinion of you. Do not give her reason to downplay your importance to her team by placing her in a position where she is uniformed or unaware of relevant issues that impact her business. The key to avoid this is

to maintain an open communication path between you and your manager. Do not take action, even if it's with good intentions, without keeping your manager informed.

What happens if you do not follow the rules of the Expectation Game? You will not earn your manager's confidence or trust. She will not see you as a vital role on her team in her organization which may affect your job security and negatively impact your career path.

Factor #5 – Fire, Jump, Throw, Duck & Weave

For the video game, understanding what the controller or joystick does allows you to understand what tools are at your disposal. For early video games, a joystick was the only toolbox available on which you could rely. It was basically a stick with a button next to it. This toolbox did not provide many tools to use. The stick moved your character around the video world and the button allowed you to fire a weapon, jump or perform other single action moves.

Today, the joystick has been replaced with a handheld controller that increases the tools available for the player. Some consoles have as many as fifteen buttons. Each one has a purpose and the player can hit a combination of buttons to access more complex tools. For example, the "O" button could be for jump, the "X" button for fire and the up arrow for run. But if the player hits all three simultaneously, they could have his character run, jump and fire all at the same time.

For Super Mario, some of the tools include jump, double jump, run, walk, throw, super smash, somersault and twirl. Mario also uses tools such as throwing coins, riding on the back of Yoshee, his green dinosaur buddy, and pouncing on the enemies' heads to disorient them before smashing them into oblivion with Yoshee's tail. The more tools the player has to call upon, the more successful they will be at winning the video game.

For the Expectations Game, employees equip themselves with their own tools. Some of the tools they might have at their disposal are their education and work experience. An employee with a degree from a renowned business school will have more tools when compared to an employee with an Associate's degree from a technical college. An employee with years of ex-

perience will have more tools to call on than one new to the workforce. Other tools that equip you as an employee are your skill sets, your contacts and support network and any proven best practices that are transferable to your new role.

Another tool is the preparation you did for the role. Preparation may be graduating from college, or interning with a similar company or completing training or certification that is mandatory for your position. Employees also have tools that come from their educational background. These may include computer software expertise, graduate education in a specific field or hands-on experience gained at a technical college.

What happens if you do not utilize your tools or find the tools in your toolbox limiting? You will be placed at a disadvantage against your coworkers who will use them to perform better and in a more efficient manner. But this is not a terminal situation. You can always add tools to your toolbox.

Factor #6 – Ouch! What Was That?

There are many obstacles in a video game. Often, a player notices the obstacle after they have been hit by it. It may be a fire ball thrown by an enemy, or a bump from a toxic foe. Depending on the game, other obstacles could be Nazis, mushroom men, spiders, volcanoes, man-eating zombies, man-eating aliens, man-eating teddy bears, man-eating flowers etc. Video game designers are a creative bunch. If the player does not overcome or outmaneuver the obstacles they will suffer damage that will decrease his energy which could result in a life loss.

For the Expectations Game, some of the obstacles that you will face as an employee include dealing with the daily responsibilities of your job, competitive co-workers, organizational silos, budget cuts, compliance procedures, competition, office politics and computer expertise. But obstacles are not limited to ones related to the education and experience you bring to your job. Other obstacles can include your ability to balance your personal life with your professional life.

What happens if you do not overcome the obstacles you face? The level of trust (support) between you and your manager may decrease, you may lose motivation (energy) to do a good job and you may have fewer opportunities (player lives) for career advancement.

Factor #7 – Gold Coins and Power Stars!

For the video game, the rewards include defeating Bowser and rescuing Princess Peach from his hidden fortress. Other rewards include achieving a high score, finding all of the Power Stars, gaining extra lives, opening new galaxies, saving the Hungry Lumas and Toad Brigade, amassing Gold Coins and Star Bits. Once complete, the player has the opportunity to play the game again with a new character but at a harder level than before, making it more challenging and rewarding.

For the Expectations Game, some of the rewards for the employee for achieving the company's goals include hitting financial targets that have monetary bonus, better performance reviews and an increase in salary. Other rewards are more intangible in nature. It could be having his manager's confidence in his abilities, projecting a positive image to upper management as a valuable asset and increasing future job security. And like the video game, once the employee successfully plays the Expectations Game, they may have a chance to play it again but at a harder level that is more challenging and rewarding such as getting promoted to a higher level of responsibility or transitioning into a more demanding work environment.

What would happen if you, as the employee, lost sight of the rewards? You would be less inclined to invest the time and resources needed to succeed. You would lose your motivation to do your job, and your attitude would go from "want to be here" to a "have to be here." Unfortunately, many employees do not realize that they do not have a choice on whether or not to play the Expectations Game. As an employee, you have a boss so you have expectations that must be met if you hope to succeed.

What would happen if you decided to explore Super Mario Galaxy without following the rules of the game? You wouldn't go very far before you were faced with an obstacle. If you were to avoid the obstacle, you would not be able to progress to the next level of responsibility and challenge. You would not complete your task and time would run out. All of these would result in your forfeiting one of your player's lives. Three lives lost and the game is over.

What would happen if you decided to not play the Expectations Game as an employee? This is the same as asking what would happen if you chose to not follow

GAME OVER

rules of your workplace. Like in the video game, you would not go very far before you were faced with an obstacle. Avoiding the obstacle would decrease the level of trust your manager has in you. You would no longer be seen as a valuable asset to the company. If you were to continue on this trend, to continue to not follow the rules, you would more than likely be fired and replaced by someone who will follow the rules.

The obstacle may be a minor assignment your manager gives you. Maybe she asks that you update the daily sales report. You decide not to do it because you're doing a weekly update tomorrow. What would happen? Your manager would become upset that you not only failed to complete a task asked of you, but, that by doing so, you questioned her judgment on what was important. This act would deteriorate the trust she has in you going forward.

What happens if you succeed at playing the Expectations Game for a little while but are unable, or unwilling, to play it for the long run? Many employees find themselves at this point in their career. He or she was able to excel at their position and play the Expectations Game which resulted in a promotion. But at this higher level of responsibility, they found themselves unable to excel at their new position, much less meet all expectations placed on them by their manager. Often, the result of this is that they will not progress further on their career path.

So what can you do tomorrow as an employee? First, recognize that there are expectations placed on you and begin to play the Expectations Game. Get some quick wins on the board by meeting your manager's most pressing expectations and she will support you when you need it. By showing your ability to do what needs to be done, as your manager sees it, you have proven yourself a valuable employee. Communicate successes as they relate to your manager's agenda on a regular basis. Reiterate what the expectations are. This shows that you are listening and understanding what she sees as the priorities for you. Express concern when goals are divergent of one another and support when they are congruent with company's goals.

Keep a few additional things in mind as you play the Expectations Game. Do not let your ego get in the way. It is human nature to give ourselves more credit than we deserve, and, when this happens, we begin to take things for granted. Suddenly, we are not playing the Expectations Game. Instead, we are playing the "We Deserve More And It Should Be Given To Us Game" which is the road to career ruin. Another tip is to become comfortable at multi-tasking many different assignments at once. This will become your go-to-skill as more demands are put on you.

You do not want to see a "Game Over" sign on your cubicle because you were not able to play the Expectations Game. And while you can always put more coins into a video game, you only get so many shots at winning the Expectations Game and having a successful career. Make the first one last by preparing yourself properly for all possible obstacles. You may never make the high score at your company, but you can make yourself a more valuable asset that is successful at achieving your company's goals and be satisfied in that achievement.

Harriett decides to expand her horizons and turns around and walks back to the video game store where her neighbor boys were locked in computer generated combat. Harriett asks the younger of the two if she might have a turn. With a shocked look on his face, he hands over the controller. Harriett doesn't know what to do with it but holds it loosely in her hands. As soon as she touches it, half of the video screen spins in circles. It appears the boys were playing a first-person shooter game and her grip caused her player to spin in circles aimlessly. Harriett hands the controller back to the dumbfounded boys, thanks them and leaves.

As Harriett walks towards her car she thinks how her lack of knowledge on how to play the video game resulted in her player spinning around aimlessly. This reminds her of her earlier thought about comparing the game of bridge to playing the Expectations Game at work. In both, she learned the rules, understood the tools, identified obstacles and pursued a reward.

Even though she was unable to control her video game player, she was able to shatter the boy's expectations of what to expect from an elderly woman. The looks on their faces when she walked away showed her that even at ninety-four years old, she is still able to exceed peoples' expectations of her.

The Toonalution of ...Managing Expectations

TOONALUTION #10 - Weighing the Cost of Peak Performance

Kathy Stewart flicks down the channels looking for Dr. Charles Stanley's First Baptist Atlanta's televised Sunday service. Typically, she would be arriving home from early church service at this time, but today, she is nursing a nasty cold that was brought on by stretching herself too thin between her personal and professional lives. She pauses briefly on a NASCAR race that is underway. Normally she would not watch any type of auto race, but the fanfare of the event catches her attention.

Kathy imagines herself racing her Honda around a high-banked NASCAR oval track in speeds excess of two hundred miles per hour. She knows the only way her Honda could reach those speeds would be if it was being pushed by the solid rocket boosters found on the space shuttle. She knows that her car couldn't hit even one hundred and fifty miles per hour without significant upgrades to its drive train, chassis and suspension systems. She also knows it couldn't reach the posted speed limits without keeping up a routine maintenance schedule. Her husband of over thirty years, Jim, recently installed new brake pads and rotors but a recent downpour showed her windshield wipers would be needed soon.

Kathy finds the *In Touch Ministries* program she was searching for. She settles in and hopes that she will be able to relax the remainder of the day. Tomorrow is the first day of the work week and, for Kathy, it is the first day for one of her three jobs. Kathy wears many hats in her career.

She has worked out of her home as an Administrative Assistant with BNA for the past nine years. She maintains data spreadsheets, compiles sales reports and processes expenses for reimbursement for forty sales representatives. She also works as an Executive Assistant for a sports lawyer at Moye Sports Associates, Inc. two days a week where she is responsible for making travel arrangements, managing the office and maintaining client information. With the remaining time during the week, she operates her own Life Coach business where she coaches clients from all types of careers. Kathy has a Bachelor of Science in Education from Belhaven College in Jackson, MS and completed her Foundational Course in Coaching at Institute for Life Coach Training under the certification of the International Coaching Federation (www.yourlife-coach.com).

Kathy is driven by her desire to help people and encourage them to be the best they can be. A Christian for many years, Kathy's greatest passion is for the Lord Jesus. She attempts to bring God pleasure by using her spiritual gifts of exhortation, service and mercy. She has demonstrated this numerous times through mission trips to Africa and her volunteer work on the Non-Resident Ministry Team (NRMT) at Perimeter Church. She and her husband were even missionaries for two years in Kenya. Kathy led bible studies and discipled two Kenyan women. Jim, an architect by trade, designed and helped build the first English speaking seminary in East Africa and oversaw other construction projects for other Christian groups in the area. While there, they raised their daughter Becca and witnessed the birth of their son, Griffin.

They have also gone on short trips to Tanzania to serve the widows and orphans of a small village, Karansi. They worked alongside their partners in the village by visiting widows and Compassion children. They spent time encouraging teachers, teaching classes on proper hygiene, child rearing and how to conduct a small business venture. They played with the children and facilitated Vacation Bible School. In Arusha, they encouraged their partners in evangelism, educated locals on AIDS and HIV prevention, conducted discipleship classes and supported the local missionaries through prayer and works of service. They have witnessed God work miracles since their first visit eight years ago.

The village of Karansi was decimated by the loss of the men to AIDS and malaria leaving the widows and orphans helpless. But today, the orphans are paired up with relatives or widows and taught agriculture and farming to help support themselves. Since the church began serving the region, there have been significant improvements including the first english medium Christian school, a drinking well, a marketplace open twice a week and the general transformation to a moral community. Since 2002, the village has grown from four thousand villagers to over eight thousand in 2010.

As the local church leader, Pastor Wariaeli Maphie led and grew his flock, more and more families moved to the village so their children could attend the Christian School. So many families moved that the district commissioner moved the regional government offices near the village to accommodate demand. Pastor Wariaeli called his children's ministry "PUNCH MI" which stood for "Poor UNeducated CHildren's MInistry. In January of 2009, 100% of seventh graders passed the standard entrance exam which was a first for the area.

Kathy and Jim have three wonderful adult children and two amazing grandchildren. Before her administrative work, Kathy was a homemaker for seventeen years. Prior to that, she taught school and worked for Delta Airlines in the reservations department and led employee event efforts. Once she coordinated the fundraising and planning for a Christmas party for over one thousand employees. Even more fulfilling was using her gifts to facilitate a tenth and twenty-fifth anniversary at her church where she authored their ten year church history.

Kathy sees herself as someone who has great people skills who genuinely cares about the whole person: spiritually, personally and professionally. Described by many as being friendly, caring, organized and hard working, Kathy's goal is to transition to a full time coaching role sometime in the future as a Life Coach, or a coach in a company helping the employees meet their goals.

Kathy's foray into being a Life Coach was a gradual process and it continues to evolve as the recession impacts the country and her business. She has always met with and mentored single women in their walks with the Lord. Becoming a Life Coach has been a natural progression from there. As a Life Coach, Kathy enjoys seeing the coaching process work in helping clients find their passion and to work towards having it front and center in their lives. The one aspect she struggles with is marketing herself to increase her client base, and she sees the need to do this as being more important in today's environment than ever before.

Kathy sees the need to upgrade her business as being similar to the need to upgrade her Honda if she were to ever take it racing. In both scenarios, there would be a cost to achieving the performance level desired. Both would take time, financial resources and significant effort. Kathy isn't sure if that is an investment she is willing to make at this time in her business. And she definitely knows she is not ready to make that kind of investment in her Honda.

The Toonalution of Kathy Stewart

In this chapter we will look at how upgrading an organization is very similar to upgrading a vehicle for a race. But, instead of being from the employee's perspective, it will be from a "Top-Down" perspective. Why? Because as an employee, it is important to understand how decisions made by upper management can affect you at your level. We will identify and discuss the seven steps involved in doing this. These steps are:

1. Mind Your DNFs and DNQs
2. Road or Rally?
3. Trees, Peeps, Rabbits and Rocks...Oh My!
4. Upgrade Parts
5. Pit Crew Revival
6. Cash or Check?
7. Victory Lane

Today, all companies find themselves in a very challenging, ever changing environment. From economic challenges to international competition to commodity price increases, the need for companies to upgrade their organizations is both broad and deep in scope. All businesses from the multinational, globalized powerhouse to the locally owned grocery store on a street corner are being impacted in one way or another. What was once a clear and steady course is now filled with new obstacles and is no longer straight and true. Only the companies that invest in upgrading their organizations to meet these new demands will be able to compete in this race. How will they do this? The first step is to realize that there is an issue that needs to be addressed.

Step #1 – Mind Your DNFs and DNQs

One of the most significant challenges in racing is to identify issues that affect a team's ability to perform. For this example, I've separated these issues into two buckets; "1987 Corvette" issues and "1955 Corvette" issues.

The 1987 Corvette issues are what would be classified as small issues that are easily fixed. The Corvette had been America's sports car for over thirty years. A new model had been successfully launched in 1984 and by 1987 most of the production bugs had been worked out. Chevrolet's plan going forward was to address issues quickly and make minor changes to keep buyers interested and visiting their showrooms. Any issues that were present could be easily addressed. This plan worked smoothly for the next ten years until the next generation Corvette was introduced in 1997.

For our racing example, a 1987 Corvette issue could be when an engine is down on horsepower because of a blown spark plug or the suspension is set up incorrectly which causes the tires to wear out prematurely. Both examples are difficult to deal with at the time, but they are easily fixed and won't cause lasting damage to the success of the team.

The 1955 Corvette issues are the big issues that affect a team's ability to operate day-to-day, much less perform well in a race. The 1955 Corvette was chosen because just two years after its introduction, it was slated to be discontinued. It was introduced in 1953 with an anemic six-cylinder engine, a chunky three-speed transmission, a high price tag and one available color combination, a white exterior with a red interior. It was far from being anyone's, much less America's, sports car. Significant investments would have to be made in order for the Corvette to sell well and be a competitive threat to other car companies.

What saved it from being discontinued? It was saved by the introduction of the 1955 Ford Thunderbird which was ironically created to compete against the Corvette. In its first year, the Thunderbird outsold the Corvette 23 to 1. This new drop-top competitor came standard with a powerful eight-cylinder engine, optional Ford-O-Matic 3-speed automatic transmission, vibrant pastel colors and an optional hardtop. It fueled Chevrolet's competitive juices enough for it to invest the needed resources into the Corvette. A temporary bandage was put in place for 1955 with the introduction of an eight-cylinder engine. The investment came to fruition in 1956 with an all-new body style that incorporated roll up windows, a V-8 engine and an optional Powerglide automatic transmission. Without this investment, America's sports car would not have the fifty-eight year history it does today.

An example of a 1955 Corvette issue would be if a racing engine is consistently down on horsepower because it is not built properly or if the suspension is never correct because of the components sourced. These are big issues that will be harder to address quickly because they involve structural changes to the racing organization. To build a better engine, mechanics may need to be retrained or replaced. To calibrate a suspension setup correctly, new suppliers may be needed that cannot be approached until contractual obligations are met.

But how does a team identify their Corvette issues? One way is by minding their DNQs and DNFs. In racing, teams must post qualifying laps on a race track to determine the starting grid. In NASCAR, the top forty-three teams with the best times qualify for the race. The teams will line up at the start of the race in order of their qualification results from the best to the worse time.

At the end of a race, if a team did not have a car that crossed the finish line, they are labeled either "DNQ" or "DNF." DNQ stands for "Did Not Qualify" and DNF stands for "Did Not Finish." While both situations are poor results for a team to experience, one is much worse than the other when trying to identify how they can improve their results.

"DNF" means that your racecar was performing well enough to qualify. You and your team were prepared to race against a field of competitors, but you were unable to sustain an adequate level of performance to finish the race. Reasons for a "DNF" include having an accident, driver error, equipment failure or running out of resources (gas).

"DNQ" means that the team's performance was so poor that they could not even qualify for the race. They were unable to even be the best of the worst. Reasons for this are the same as for a DNF but with a greater chance of being related to equipment failure or the team's inability to compete. The issues involved are usually 1955 Corvette issues that cannot be easily fixed without a significant investment of time and resources.

It is easier for a team to identify 1955 Corvette issues if they consistently have DNQs. Why? Because if a team is not able to qualify for a race, it is obvious they have a big issue. They are missing the mark on numerous fronts whether it is financial backing, part sourcing or team experience. These are the teams that know they have to address their 1955 Corvette issues if they hope to make a course correction soon and improve their results.

A team that consistently has DNFs may not realize that they have 1955 Corvette issues that must be addressed. Why? Because the small successes they do have, qualifying and finishing some races, can mask many issues and give them a false sense of confidence. Their ability to see the need for a course correction is blinded by the minor successes they experience. If you were the team owner, would you want to invest significant resources into what you view as a 1987 Corvette situation? It takes strong leadership to identify the real issues and act against them. Especially in an organization that is showing some results.

For a company, the same issues can present themselves. The finish line for a company would be the time in which they can quantify their progress against set goals. Financial finish lines can be identified during quarterly, mid-year and annual earnings statements. Competitive finish lines can be identified through market share changes and the ability to address new consumer trends.

A DNQ for a company would be one that is unable to succeed on any level. This could be the local restaurant that cannot draw in customers. Their 1955 Corvette issue may be location, poor offerings or the results from a health inspection. Some of these issues are easier to fix than others, but all are difficult.

A DNF for a company would be where financial targets are not met or fall short of investor's expectations. A majority of publicly-traded companies fall in this category. Often, valid reasons are given for not making the targets. There might be price pressures from new overseas competition, or a freeze in the credit markets that limit operating cash flow to pressure from an aggressive majority share holder. These issues are not new and they will always be around. Their 1955 Corvette issues may be an inability to adjust to commodity fluctuations or an aggressive competitor that is quick to provide new offerings to consumers.

Like the racing example, a DNF is a situation where it might be harder for the company's upper management to identify the need for a course correction. The quarterly targets that are hit mask the miss three months earlier. The upward tick in the stock price overshadows the fundamentals that keep the company from achieving top-tiered growth.

Most companies find themselves needing to make improvements just to keep pace, much less to improve their performance. There is a danger that these ongoing minor improvements will cloud judgment. Upper management may feel that since they are already investing in their business that they are being proactive enough and do not need to do anything else. But if their investments are directed towards the wrong goal, resources will be wasted. This would be like replacing the shocks on your car but never changing the oil. Sure it will be a smooth ride, but only until your engine blows up.

Without improvements, a company will be unable to react to unforeseen obstacles. If not addressed the company will lose market share, sales will decline and profit margins will decrease. To better illustrate this, let's look at how your average company would fare in a race.

Today, the majority of companies can look at themselves as a semi tractor-trailer truck racing around on an oval race track. This imagery is being used to show the impact complacency, by operating at status quo, can have on a company's ability to remain competitive. This complacency will make a company heavy, slow and unable to make changes quickly. Up until now, most companies have survived by maintaining the same basic practices they have always operated under. The oval track is easy, predictable and without many surprises. A semi tractor-trailer truck is able to navigate it because even though it is large, heavy and unable to make quick moves, it is not asked to. While it cannot handle chicanes or changes to the racetrack, it can handle the large, long sweepers and straight-aways.

What would happen if a sharp turn were added to the track? The truck would initially hesitate, and then make adjustments to tackle the curve. It would slow down to take it cautiously. Its load would shift and its contents could become damaged. Additional strain would be placed on the suspension that would shorten its ability to perform and give the competition an opening in which to pass.

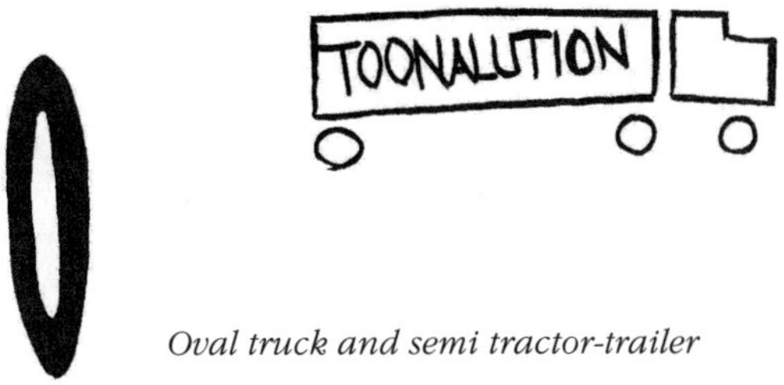

Oval truck and semi tractor-trailer

While the truck will make it through the curve, it will struggle every time. The demand will slow its overall performance and wear down its systems. It will shorten the life cycle of the truck and increase its operating costs. If it is expected to perform at a competitive level on this new track, significant changes need to be made to address its long-term sustainability.

Just like the truck trying to remain on the racetrack, most companies today are finding themselves competing on a new race track. Their track may have many new curves in it. The turns in the track could be issues such as a recessed global economy, aggressive competition, a shift in consumer demand or internal issues such as a poorly communicated company vision, inadequate corporate governance or an inability to utilize new technological advances. In order to perform well, the company must invest in itself to improve its performance level while weighing the costs associated with implementation.

Step #2 – Road or Rally?

Our truck has left the oval course and finds itself on a new racetrack with new demands. It is no longer on an oval track with long straight-aways and high-banked curves. It is on a track that is similar to a rally track. Rallying, racing on a rally track, is a very popular sport in Europe and South America. It has recently become popular in the United States and is a regular event at the X Games where Ford Focuses, Mitsubishi Evos, Citroen C4s and Subaru Imprezas can be found performing acrobatic moves typically seen in motocross events.

Unlike most racetracks, rally tracks are dirt roads that serpentine through dense forest and villages. The tracks are framed by trees, rocks, buildings, spectators and an occasional wayward animal. Rally races are not delayed because of weather, occur during the day and night and are often accompanied by the sounds of splintering wood and rattling suspensions as drivers fly by letting their wheels touch ground just enough to stay on course.

Because of the dangers involved in rallying, the cars are highly customized to overcome these obstacles. And all of these upgrades come with financial sacrifices. They take the cost per car from the stock price of around $35k to upwards of $1M.

Companies today are trying to navigate on a high-speed, tree-lined, rock-laden, critter-accompanied, dirt rally track. Gone are the wide straight-aways of predictable earning and strong operating margins, the banked curves of satisfied consumers and unassertive competitors and the stability of a semi tractor-trailer that is only asked to keep the headlights pointed straight.

What would happen if this eighteen-wheeler attempted to race on a high-

Rally track added

speed, tree-lined, rock-laden, critter-accompanied, dirt rally track? It wouldn't make the first turn much less complete the race. Its weight would make it unable to get up to speed, its mass would force it to take corners slowly and its suspension would be pushed past its limits to total system failure. Its headlights wouldn't be able to penetrate the dust clouding forward vision and the truck would be in danger of complete failure.

It seems ridiculous for a truck like this to attempt to race in a rally but many companies today are doing just that. Instead of literally spinning their wheels in the mud, they are losing market share to their competitors, reacting slowly to consumer or technological shifts or becoming clouded in their vision and purpose.

What happens if this company stays on its current path? They will not be able to meet current or future demands, they will miss their financial commitments and productivity will decline as operating costs go up. The company will have to change direction if they hope to continue and compete successfully. So we now know we must upgrade our company, our truck into a rally car, to compete on this new high-speed, tree-lined, rock-laden, critter-accompanied, dirt rally track, but how do we do that?

Step #3 – Trees, Peeps, Rabbits and Rocks...Oh My!

This new high-speed, tree-lined, rock-laden, critter-accompanied, dirt rally track has obstacles that, while not being new, are coming towards our rally car at a faster pace than what the driver may be accustomed to. That small pebble or piece of rubber that was a nuisance on the oval track is now a boulder that is bouncing towards the driver at a high speed. He not only has to be aware of the obstacles, he has to be able to communicate them to his pit crew and overcome them. If he and his team do not make adjustments to the rally car, they will struggle to overcome the obstacle every time they experience it.

Some obstacles such as a driver's people/supporters (peeps) are positive factors that can become obstacles if the rally car is unable to stay on course. Positive or not, they are factors that need to be considered when racing.

Other obstacles which may have been unforeseen before on an oval track that are now visible on a high-speed, tree-lined, rock-laden, critter-accompanied, dirt rally track would include wild animals, rocks, dirt and debris, spectators, trees and bushes.

Similarly, companies today are facing new obstacles at a faster pace. Like a pebble that is now a large boulder, a company may face an aggressive competitor who once was not a credible threat to its business. An example of this is eBay's affect on traditional brick-and-mortar stores. Originally designed as an online auction house, eBay quickly transformed itself into a virtual shopping mall selling everything from children's clothing to automobiles to a chance to be a character in a book. Users were able to set up their own virtual store fronts that allowed them to sell new and used items directly to their customers. According to eBay's financial results, their net revenue went from $5.7 million in 1997 to $8.7 billion in 2009. They went from being a pebble in 1997 to a boulder in 2009. Traditional stores have had to invest in improvements in order to remain competitive. This could be through creating their own website to sell their goods or by selling products on eBay itself.

Trees, Peeps, Rabbits and Rocks...added

Companies must identify their obstacles and communicate them throughout its upper management so solutions can be identified and implemented. If this is not done, the company will struggle to overcome these obstacles every time they experience them. By upgrading the company, it will be able to overcome the obstacles it has been either avoiding or hitting straight on. Both slow a company's progress or inflict damage which increases its operating costs to fix. For a company these obstacles could be the financial indicators they have been missing, or its ability to hire and retain quality employees or its ability to change as its consumers' demands change.

Step #4 – Upgrade Parts

As the driver and his pit crew recognize that they are on a more difficult track with more obstacles to overcome, they realize that they need to invest in upgrading their vehicle to be competitive. But which parts should they discard and upgrade and which parts should they keep? For a rally car there are numerous systems that can be upgraded.

For more power, the drive train, also known as a power train, must be upgraded. The drive train includes the engine, transmission, driveshaft, differentials and universal joint. Within these components are additional parts such as the pistons, carburetor and fuel pump for the engine or the clutch plate, gears and shifter for the transmission.

Parts upgraded

For a company, there are many systems that must be upgraded as well to keep a competitive edge. For more power, a company could upgrade its talent by hiring graduates with degrees in higher education, launching new training initiatives or offering reimbursement for continuing education courses.

For better handling, the suspension and steering systems must be upgraded. These systems include the shock absorbers, springs, torsion bars, struts, rack &

pinion, tie rods and steering arms. Another way to improve handling is to reduce the vehicle's weight and to expand its track width which will reduce its center of gravity.

For better handling, a company could improve its decisions-making process by reducing layers of management, by streamlining and clarifying its communication path or by organizing Business Units so they are more accountable to sales results.

For better traction, the aerodynamics, the tires/wheels and brake systems must be upgraded. Aerodynamics includes spoilers, splitters and wings you often see on overly accessorized imports with oversized mufflers that are often heard before they are seen. These accessories help minimize wind resistance by channeling wind around, over and under the vehicle. This increases the rally car's down force which will keep its tires in greater contact with the track, thus increasing traction.

The other systems include tires, wheels, brake pads, master cylinder, rotors, discs, calipers and actuators. Most of these can be upgraded in size, width or materials to increase grip and shorten braking distances.

For better visibility, the lighting and visibility systems must be upgraded. This system includes the headlights, roof light bar, windshield, wipers, mirrors, and visors. Visibility can be increased by adding additional lights or upgrading current lighting to be more effective. The mirrors, visors and windshield can be treated to reduce glare and increase visibility.

Each of these systems can be replaced by better performing parts that may be more efficient, lighter or more durable than the parts they replace. But each part comes at an additional cost to the team that must be weighed against the projected benefits and the loss of a working part. An increase in durability is often accompanied by an increase in cost and weight. A decrease in weight also comes with an increase in cost and usually a decrease in durability.

A company could increase its traction by investing in new products, expanding its marketing and advertising programs and investing in new revenue streams. For more visibility, upper management could communicate its vision and mission statement throughout the entire organization, align departments for more transparency to its investors and invest additional dollars in sales data so it could identify competitor advances earlier.

All of these efforts would involve the upgrading of parts to the company's "rally car". These parts include manufacturing plants, production facilities, equipment, intellectual data and employees.

Step #5 – Pit Crew Revival

The role of the pit crew is just as important to the success of running a race as the driver and rally car. Today, the pit crew is defined as the crew members who actively participate in race. In the past, pit crews also included all of the mechanics and fabricators involved in preparing a car for race day. For this example, we will include them as well. A typical pit crew has anywhere from 25 to 60 members depending on the team's racing budget. In addition to the mechanics and fabricators who build the racecar, the pit crew has a Crew Chief, a Pit Crew Coach, a Jackman, Front and Rear Tire Changers, a Gas Man, a Gas Catch Man, and Front and Rear Tire Carriers. While these crew members are busiest on race day, they typically assist during the week in preparing the race car. NASCAR limits the number of pit crew members active on race day to seven while Formula 1 allows up to eighteen. In 2002, Toyota had upwards of 600 employees, including fabricators and engineers, preparing two cars for entry into its first Formula 1 season.

Each crew member has a specific role to fulfill in preparation for and during a race. It is the Crew Chief's responsibility to hire and train crew members that can perform at the highest level of competition and in concert with their teammates.

The driver is responsible for executing the team's plan and communicating opportunities for improvement. As he competes in the race, he communicates any issues he is having with the racecar. As the conditions change on the race track, he tells his pit crew what adjustments he believes they need to execute to compensate. For example, if the track is slippery because of the afternoon sun, the pit crew would tighten up the suspension system to give the driver more feedback on what the tires are doing via the steering wheel. Or, if the driver prefers to race at a high line on the track, he may request an adjustment to the camber of the tires to make it easier to maintain his line.

Like a pit crew, a company must have a team managing its performance to make sure it is competitive on race day. Instead of a Crew Chief leading, companies have an Executive Team that operates at the direction of the Chief Executive Officer (CEO). It is the Executive Team's job to drive the company forward in attaining its goals. They must navigate the company around obstacles and its competition. Instead of directing tire changers and mechanics, the Executive Team directs the company's upper management team and business unit leaders. Upper management would be the leaders of the major divisions within a company including Sales, Logistics, Human Resources and Marketing. They are the crew members who help build a better company. They act on the Executive Team's directions and execute their plans to increase performance and achieve goals.

Driver added

The driver of the rally car is the CEO who is charged with driving the company towards the identified goals. She, or he, with the help of the Executive Team, must build a rally car that is competitive (power), able to make changes quickly (handling), able to overtake competitors (traction) and able to see upcoming obstacles and challenges (visibility). And like a NASCAR driver who must perform well in order to secure funding from his advertisers, the CEO must perform well for the company to be seen as a wise investment to shareholders. While a driver's responsibility may include wearing sponsor's logos on his suit, attending corporate events and maintaining a positive image, a CEO's responsibilities are more involved. Their responsibilities include providing value to their investors, superior services or products and operating honestly in dealing with their employees, customers and clients. Sometimes these responsibilities may seem to be in conflict with each other. But realize that often operating honestly means telling employees, customers and clients information they do not want to hear such as missed projections, downsizing initiatives or plant closures.

Who are you as an employee? You are a part of the corporate "rally team". Everyone, whether you are a director of sales, an account manager or a fork lift operator is a necessary part that must perform his job functions well. Ask yourself, are you a high performing part that will easily fit within the new rally team structure? Or, are you an inefficient part that needs to be replaced? If you feel you are an outdated two-barrel carburetor that has a hard time starting in the morning, reference Toonalution #6 to become the employee you desire to be.

Like a driver communicates opportunities to his pit crew, a CEO needs to listen to her employees to communicate opportunities to her upper management. Why do companies not solicit feedback? Because there are so many different parts of the organization that the feedback received is often not actionable or focused. For every actionable comment received there will be many more that are not. This may be because an employee uses the forum to express their opinions on other topics or they do not have complete knowledge of the situation. Good companies establish a forum for idea sharing or a process to upwardly feed comments through its management structure.

Step #6 – Cash or Check?

So far, we've shown how companies need to assess their performance (Mind Your DNFs & DNQs), are competing on a new track (Road or Rally?), with new obstacles (Trees, Peeps, Rabbits and Rocks…Oh My!), that necessitate a need to invest in upgrading its organization (Upgrade Parts) to build a stronger organization (Pit Crew Revival). But what are the costs involved in accomplishing these endeavors?

There are two types of costs: known and unknown. Please, take a moment to wrap your brain around this amazing concept. The known costs are ones that are easily captured on a financial balance sheet and can be quantified. The unknown costs are not easily captured but affect performance and must be considered as part of the decision-making process.

The known costs will vary based on what kind of race car and track a company is today compared to where it wants to be. Is your company a semi tractor-trailer that is racing on a rally track? Or is your company a rally car that only needs minor upgrades to be competitive in today's environment?

For both a race team and a company, the known costs are similar. Both include the staffing and training of employees and the operation of offices and assets. While a race team would incur additional expenses for the replacement of an unproductive part with a new, more efficient part, a company would incur additional expenses for eliminating or outsourcing an under producing, or costly, employee or department. There are costs associated with moving or closing a facility and the laying off of employees

Like a race team that replaces its four barrel Holley carburetor with an Edelbrock fuel injection system that increases performance and improves gas mileage, a company may invest in external recruiting firms to upgrade its workforce. Both have potential for increasing performance but both also come with inherent risks. The new fuel injection system may have a break in period that limits horsepower in the short-term; the company's current workforce may feel threatened by a new class of educated, inexperienced employees.

Unknown costs are ones that cannot be quantified or are unforeseen results from the restructuring. Again, the costs are similar for both a race team and a company. These can include the relationships they have with their sponsorship, advertisers, customers and investors. Unknown costs could be a slippage in performance because focus is redirected towards efforts to upgrade the organization. One of the most impactful unknown costs is the lowering of employee morale. If left unchecked, this unknown cost will affect a company's ability to perform which may outweigh any projected revenue associated with upgrading the organization.

One example of known and unknown costs can be seen with Ford Motor Company's restructuring efforts beginning in 2007. Ford found itself racing on the wrong track to profitability losing $12.7 billion in 2006. Ford was in a "1955 Corvette" situation. They were not meeting financial expectations that were beginning to threaten the stability of the entire company.

Realizing that aggressive efforts were needed, in February of 2007, the news organization Reuters reported that Ford Motor Company implemented a restructuring plan, dubbed "Way Forward," that would cost over $11 billion. The plan included close to $6 billion for worker reduction programs, another $3 billion for pension-related charges, $2 billion for fixed-asset impairment charges and $281 million associated with plant idling. These were the known costs associated with upgrading their organization.

How does this relate to our rally car example? It means that Ford decreased its number of employees (worker reduction programs) and retiree benefits (pension-related charges), wrote off assets (impairment charges) and closed plants as demand for their cars and trucks declined. By doing this, Ford increased its handling by reducing operating costs by downsizing its workforce and idling underutilized plants. These actions increased its power by reinforcing its financial stability by reducing the cost per vehicle. Ford increased its traction by reinvesting resources into profitable markets such as China and South America and by expanding their product line with new alternative energy offerings. They also increased their visibility by holding Business Units accountable to the CEO during their weekly Business Plan Review held in Ford's "Thunderbird Room" in Dearborn, Michigan.

As the recession impacted the economy in 2008 Ford found itself in a unique situation. While the recession negatively impacted all automobile companies, Ford continued with its restructuring plan even though they posted negative net income results. Ironically, Ford's implementation of its "Way Forward" plan in 2007 gave them the financial buffer so they would not have to take any government bailout money. As a result, Ford was the recipient of positive public relations.

Ford implemented this restructuring plan at the financial cost over $11 billion with hopes of returning to profitability by 2009. According to Ford's 2009 Full Year results, they achieved their plan by posting their first full year of positive net income since 2005 of $2.7 billion. With losses of $14.7 billion in 2008 and $2.7 billion in 2007 along with the $12.7 billion loss that triggered the restructuring plan, Ford is a long way from reaching the finish line. But they are competing with a better racecar than what they had in 2006. Ford's known costs were quantifiable and identified on its earning statements for investors. Only time, and a succession of positive financial statements, will tell if this restructuring plan has worked. Initial results are positive as they are outpacing their competition. The only unknown is whether the racecar Ford built has the endurance to continue the race to profitability.

The unknown costs from this example may include damage to Ford's employee morale from the worker reduction program, a loss of new talent by reducing potential retiree benefits or issue with product supply by closing plants. However, many of these unknown costs may be offset by the positive PR Ford received by not taking a government loan even though that result was unplanned.

Unfortunately, because unknown costs are not quantifiable on a financial balance sheet, they are not properly weighed against known costs during a company's decision-making process. This usually results with the company having to deal with them at a later date because they negatively impact the company's results. By not factoring them earlier, the cost to the company becomes greater as the issues do not become recognizable until they are significant.

One way a company protects themselves is by knowing the approximate pay and benefit packages offered by their competitors. By knowing this information, a company is able to increase its return on investment by maintaining a "competitive package" for their industry. As economies grow and shrink, companies that are able to grow and shrink their employee packages with it will be more successful that those that do not. As you would expect, companies tend to shrink faster than they grow.

Step #7 – Victory Lane

So what does a company receive for upgrading their rally car? They will be more competitive on the racetrack on which they compete. Their handling will increase allowing them to address changes in the marketplace quicker; their power will increase giving them more leverage to invest in new products and initiatives; they will have more traction allowing them to overtake competitors and increase revenue and market share, and they will have more visibility to see future trends and obstacles. All of these working in conjunction will help the company make its financial targets which will make it a more attractive investment vehicle to its shareholders, investor, customers and consumers.

Results are not guaranteed. Just like our earlier example where you replaced your shocks but didn't change the oil, there is the danger that an investment in upgrading will not be as effective as planned because it is not directed in the correct area.

For most publically traded companies, the next finish line is only thirteen weeks away at the end of the fiscal quarter. But a quarterly close should never be identified as a finish line. Winning quarterly races result in implementing business practices that work in the short-term but tend to sacrifice long-term health. A quick win on the balance sheet because cheaper ingredients were purchased for a product does not capture the long-term affect of losing customers to a competitor that makes a product with better ingredients.

Rather, quarterly closes should be a performance checkpoint in the race. The finish line should be the three or five year plan outlined by the CEO that has identifiable targets to pursue.

Kathy Stewart leaves work having recovered from the cold that kept her home on Sunday. She was thankful for the rest as well as the insight she received by watching a NASCAR race. Until that point, Kathy would have never correlated upgrading her Life Coach business to upgrading her Honda if she wanted to ever take it racing. She found it amazing the different places one could find inspiration.

Even though Kathy does not want to invest in her Honda to transform it into a high speed racecar, she realizes that there is a need to continually invest in routine maintenance. So far, it has proven to be reliable transportation for many years. And now, as she drives home from work and notices a front of dark clouds approaching, she realizes another investment in her Honda is coming soon. The cloud along with her lingering cough is prompting Kathy to make a stop for windshield wipers and a decongestant. A Pep Boys and Rite-Aid are on her way but Kathy wishes there was a one-stop alternative, such as a Pep-Aid store, to address her windshield & nose wiping needs. This investment will ensure both she and her Honda will be working at peak performance in the morning.

The Toonalution of ...Driving for Results

TOONALUTION #10 - Staying Put in the Right Role

Darren MacGillivray calls Jake, his eight year old golden retriever, inside as he prepares for a training ride on his Felt road bike. Jake is the youngest and most exuberant, of the three dogs which include Min Pins Casey and Duke.

Darren has always maintained a very athletic lifestyle participating in every type of event including triathlons, marathons and Ironman competitions. He also volunteers as the Chairman of the Fitness Committee at the local Yacht Club where he was able to guide the revamping of their fitness center. One of his favorite activities is running alongside his son, Christian, as he races his Lightning McQueen big boy bike down the street.

Recently, Darren began an aggressive workout schedule in preparation for an upcoming competition. Some recent competitions include the Coeur d' Alene in 2008 and the Lake Placid Ironman in 2010. All Ironman competitions consist of a 2.4 mile swim, a 112 mile bike ride and a 26.2 mile marathon. Darren completed each event in 12:22:14 and 12:00:42 respectively which beat his initial goal of finishing in under thirteen hours.

In 2006, Darren participated in an International Distance Triathlon in which he was paired with a disabled athlete in support of the C Different Foundation. This organization "was founded to inspire visually impaired people around the world to lead active and healthy lives." His partner, Dave Bigoney, lost his sight during a domestic violence episode with his stepmother in which he sustained a gunshot wound to his head and his father was murdered. Darren and Dave completed the triathlon crossing the finish line together. Because of demands of competing in athletic events, Darren credits the support of his wife, Cheryl, with his ability to participate and considers them family events.

Darren graduated from the University of Georgia with a Bachelor of Science and Geography in 1992. While there, he attended Air Force ROTC with hopes to join the military to pursue a career as a pilot. But as all military branches drew down the number of recruits because of the fall of the Berlin Wall, opportunities were limited. Darren had to pursue his career through the civilian route and enrolled in Flight School at Comair Aviation Academy in Orlando. He eventually became a flight instructor and then a turbo prop pilot. Darren moved from Orlando to Cincinnati to pilot a Canadair Regional Jet which allowed him to gain experiences in flying in snow, sleet and ice.

In July of 1998, Darren participated in a two-stage interview with American Airlines that consisted of simulator training, psychological evaluation, multiple interviews as well as hearing and cognitive tests, blood work and a physical. Once completed, he nervously waited with other candidates for placement into a new hire class. At the time, American Airlines was the airline to work for with many prestigious recruits including space shuttle commander, Kurt Brown.

Darren received a call from the VP of Flight, Cecil Ewell, in September to congratulate him on being accepted and assigned as a 727 Flight Engineer in Miami. Darren quickly progressed to a 767 International First Officer on a route to destinations including Paris, Madrid, South & Central America and the Caribbean.

Each pilot in the cockpit has a different title. The Captain is the ranking pilot and is in sole command of the aircraft, passengers and crew. The First Officer (FO), or Co-Pilot, is second in command. If required, on flights longer than eight hours a third pilot designated First Officer B (FB) is assigned to provide relief and rest for the Captain and FO.

The FB is jokingly called First Break because they take the first break on an intercontinental flight. For flights over twelve hours, a fourth pilot called the First Officer C, or FC, is assigned to further enhance safety for long haul flying. They are also known as the Film Critic because they are known to burn time by watching an in-air movie with the passengers.

On 12/22/01, Darren was the FO on intercontinental Flight #63 from Paris to Miami when a Flight Attendant called the cockpit because a passenger was lighting matches in what appeared to be an attempt to smoke a cigarette. Her call quickly became a cry for help as the passenger became physically aggressive and bit her. Everyone realized that the passenger was attempting to harm himself and possibly others. They subdued him by hogtying him to his seat with headphone cords, seat belt extenders, business ties and plastic handcuffs. No one knew it at the time, but they had just subdued Richard Reid, the terrorist who became known as the Shoe Bomber, so called because he was attempting to ignite explosives hidden in his shoes.

Operating as an ETOPS aircraft, AA63 was able to fly up to 180 minutes from a suitable landing strip in order to provide more direct routing. ETOPS stands for Extended Range Twin Operations or "Engines Turn or People Swim." When Richard Reid was tied to his seat, AA63 was at this point three hours from any potential airstrip and the worst place to be during an emergency. They were in oceanic airspace, and it was decided that they would push on to United States' airspace. As they approached the U.S., Air Force F-15s were sent out to meet them to determine if they were a threat to the United States. Darren had to speak clearly to controllers to prevent any misunderstandings that could result in offensive military action.

It was later found that the terrorist was wearing four times the explosive power that brought down PAN AM 103 over Lockerbie, Scotland on December 21, 1988, killing 270 people. By the time he was subdued, the terrorist had lit over fifteen matches. The detonation cord did not ignite because of moisture from his sweaty shoes. He had been denied access the day before because of security concerns including his lack of luggage or change of clothing for an overseas trip. Despite the concerns, the airline put him up in a local hotel and rescheduled him for Flight #63 the following morning. The overnight stay coupled with his lack of clothing forced him to wear the same shoes in which moisture built up giving the crew enough time to take action.

Darren's actions during the crisis revolved around one thought: what would he do if his family were onboard? His motivation to safely transport passengers has always been fueled by this one, singular thought.

Being a natural competitor, Darren sometimes finds his role as a pilot frustrating. Because he is in a "static role," a role that an employee remains in for the majority of his or her career, staying motivated can be challenging at times. Darren knows his career path will only go as far as the Captain's chair and his frustration is compounded because he is not able to flex his competitive muscles in his professional life. Career progression in the airline industry is not based on individual performance but instead on seniority. Seniority, not job performance, determines who is promoted to Captain or the next class of jet.

However, flying is a very dynamic and demanding job: no two flights are exactly the same. Challenges in this static but dynamic job comes in many forms such as changing weather, aircraft systems malfunctions, passenger disruptions, fatigue, controller errors and sabotage threats. Any one can turn a normal day into an emergency. Also, as hard as it is to get a pilot job at a major airline, it's even harder to keep it. Every nine months, American Airline pilots are required to attend recurrent training at the "School House" in Dallas.

Recurrent training is five days of "drinking from a fire hose" including total aircraft systems, emergency procedures, aircraft limitations reviews and simulator training. It culminates with an oral examination and simulator check ride. Each year a handful of pilots are unable to maintain the rigid standards and lose their jobs. Then there are Bi-Annual medical examinations and spot checks by FAA examiners and failure to maintain standards could result in termination. Even though performance does not drive promotions, it does drive a long career and, more importantly, non-performance can be lethal.

Exploring new destinations was an initial draw for Darren towards aviation. This, along with changing routes and exercising while away, has helped him fight complacency. In February of 2001, Darren began flying a Boeing 777, or Triple 7, internationally to Buenos Aries, San Paulo, London and Madrid. After 9/11, he transitioned between different classes of airplanes because a fleet type was discontinued which displaced pilots and stewardesses who were reassigned based on seniority. Recently, Darren has enjoyed his domestic assignment flying between Los Angeles, New York, Chicago, San Francisco and Miami because it allows him to spend more time with his family.

Darren finishes preparing for his training ride which, today, is 100 miles long. He reviews his route and packs the necessary supplies including four bottles of sports drink, energy gel, two Cliff bars, spare tire tubes and CO2 and his iPhone. The challenge of endurance training and racing is much like his job: months and years of training are rewarded on race day (or on a day when an airplane engine fails), not on a daily or quarterly basis. An entire career can pass with no emergencies; the reward comes in the knowledge that you were prepared.

As Darren heads out on his ride in the sweltering ninety five degree heat, he looks enviously at his neighbor who is taking his Suzuki 650S motorcycle out for a road trip. At times, especially now, Darren wishes he could do the same.

The Toonalution of Darren MacGillivray

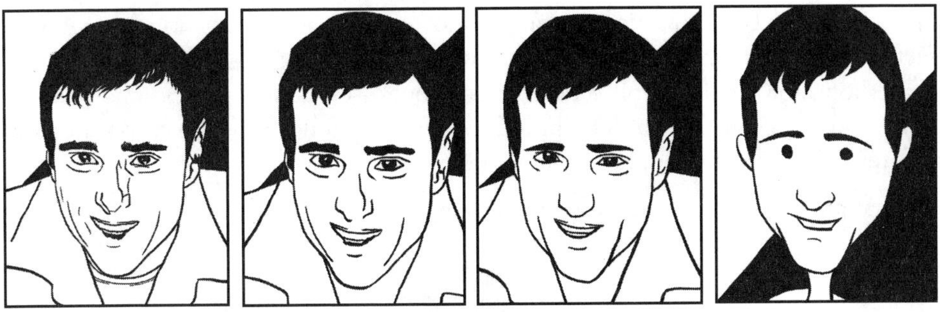

As an employee, why would you decide to stay in one position for the entire length of your career? There are many different reasons. You could be in a role that has minimal opportunity for advancement. A few examples include a musician, an airline pilot or an assembly line worker. Or you may not want the additional stress, schedule demands and responsibilities that go along with a promotion. Or you may have family obligations that are manageable within your current schedule. You may be in your dream job, your "right role," in which you find true job satisfaction. Whatever the reason, know that remaining in a role does not mean that you can stop performing above and beyond your peers. Why? Because at some point during your career, you will be measured against your peers and you do not want to be found wanting. You do not want to be seen to have less asset value to your company than your coworker. The reason, be it budget cuts, downsizing due to technological advances or other reasons, does not matter. What does matter is that you do not find yourself at the bottom of the performance pile.

Deciding to remain in your "right role," your static role, needs to be more than a settlement statement proclaimed silently through indecisiveness and inaction. As an employee, you will need to overcome numerous obstacles which include enhancing your asset value to your company, maintaining a positive attitude during times of trial, remaining challenged professionally and overcoming boredom brought on by performing repetitive tasks.

For the purposes of this chapter, I have grouped union and non-union positions together. While it can be argued that union employees do not have to worry about competition because of seniority clauses, I'm assuming that all employees, union and non-union, face the same challenges present in occupying a static position. Also, I argue that the desire to do a better job, to take a path of continual learning, is not strictly for the non-union employee who is worried about performing in a competitive environment. In fact, at times a union environment can be one that is even more difficult because of regulations that are put in place with good intentions but inhibit productivity when put into practice.

So what motivates a "static" employee? Other than the obvious ones, money, health and retirement benefits, many static employees are motivated by their lifestyle choices. They may find themselves in a good paying job with decent hours and a boss that is fair and do not want to move on to another position where those factors are unknown. This example shows that the fear of change is also a common motivator. Other employees are static because of their professional calling. For example, a musician or a computer technician cannot progress to positions of greater responsibility without additional education and experience.

What are some of the concerns with being a static employee? Over time, complacency and boredom may set in because the employee is not being challenged by new assignments and opportunities or is not learning new skills. The newness of the position is gone and they find themselves in execution mode which becomes repetitive as their career progresses. But all employees will pursue ways to make their working day more productive. The watch out is when "more productive" becomes "easier." The average worker would find their pace, set work standards that are acceptable to themselves and their manager and coast from there on. Static employees may begin watching the time clock, working the system for longer or more frequent breaks or by finding ways to do just enough to get by. The danger is that these practices will cultivate a culture of employee against employer which will lower moral, increase workplace stress and hurt productivity.

So how can you, as a static employee, improve your standing so you remain a positive and productive asset to your company? We will illustrate how you can do this by comparing a motorcycle road trip to how a static employee can go on a "Work Road Trip." This comparison includes the following steps:

1. Map Your Route
2. Call Mickey or Harry
3. Pack the Saddlebags
4. Eat, Sleep, Drink, Move On
5. Wheelies, Stoppies and Knee Draggin
6. Drafting's not just for NASCAR and Architects

Step #1 – Map Your Route

What do you do when you plan a road trip? You identify where you are going, the route you are going to take with plans for stops for food, rest and relief. Your trip may be a leisurely ride through the mountains or one to visit friends and family. Either way, you will need to plot your course so you can accomplish your goals for the ride. Even for those of you who just "Get on your hog and ride," you typically know of a destination and the general route that will get you there.

By mapping your route, you will be able to schedule necessary stops for food, rest and relief. You will be able to estimate how long your trip will take and incorporate additional tourist destinations that may be along the way such as the Air Force Museum in Dayton, Ohio, the House Inside a Redwood Log in St. Augustine, Florida, or the World of Coca Cola in Atlanta, Georgia. By planning your route you will be able to visit entertaining and educational stops that will make your trip more enjoyable for all involved.

What does it mean to map your route as an employee in a static role? Mapping your route is the same as planning your day, week or month. By planning your schedule, you will be better prepared to incorporate additional "tourist destinations" which will help you be more productive, minimize boredom and protect you from becoming complacent which will ensure that you remain a valued asset to your company.

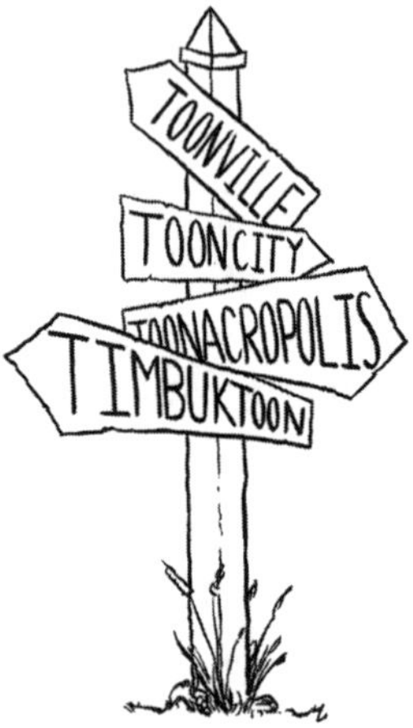

Mapping your route means to plan your day, week or month in such a way that you are able to perform your job and incorporate additional tourist destinations. Many employees use different tools such as a planner or tasks list that helps organize tasks by priority from highest to lowest. I keep a running "TTD" (Things to Do) list for weekly and monthly goals as well as other reminders that are not as time sensitive like routine chores. By planning your schedule, mapping your route, you will remove some of the daily pressures of your static role; thereby allowing you to focus your efforts on visiting new tourist destinations. This first step is key to ensuring your "Work Road Trip" starts off on the right foot, or tire, in our case.

Step #2 – Call Mickey or Harry

Visiting tourist destinations is a sure way to break up the monotony of a road trip and it can be an entertaining way to learn as well. Whether it's going to Orlando to see Mickey Mouse and Harry Potter or to the Smithsonian in Washington, you need to know the hours it is open and the costs involved. For example, tours of Frank Lloyd Wright's residential masterpiece, Falling Water, is booked months in advance and costs anywhere from $8 to walk around it to $202 for the Twilight Tour with dinner. Tickets to visit the Washington Monument are free but given out each morning and not throughout the day. If not planned properly, your visit may end at the ticket booth. Be sure to identify what you want to do and prepare properly for it.

What would be some "Tourist Destinations" as an employee in a static role? Tourist Destinations would be any activity that takes you away from your daily routine. It can be, but doesn't have to be, educational. It could be a long lunch with your spouse, or a quick game of Sudoku with your cubemate or quiet time in the break room reading a book. Or it could be learning from a coworker who is in a division that interacts with yours. If you do not plan your day, week or month properly, you may miss out on one of these Tourist Destinations. You may miss lunch with your spouse because of a forgotten meeting. Or you may forget to bring the book you want to read. Or your coworker may be attending an offsite meeting the week you wish to work with them.

A Tourist Destination can be another job at your company. For a trumpet player, maybe it's transferring from the symphony to the jazz ensemble. For a pilot, it could be moving from a trans-continental route to a domestic one. If you are an assembly line worker it may be moving to a different production station. If you are in a union role, visiting a Tourist Destination by switching roles may not be possible without a loss of income that is tied to those job functions. Whatever your situation, be sure to incorporate some "Tourist Destinations" into your "Work Road Trip".

Step #3 – Pack the Saddlebags

What is one of the first things you do before going on a road trip? If you are like most of us, you pack everything you will need while you're away. College students headed to Panama City for Spring Break pack a little differently than grandparents visiting their grandkids for Christmas. However, both parties will pack clothes, food and toiletries. Where one group may pack Flip Flops, Cheetos and Pabst Blue Ribbon, the other may pack Depends, dried prunes and Desitin. For a motorcycle road trip, items will have to fit into a tank bag, backpack or saddlebags.

The better you pack, the better prepared you will be during your trip. I've gone on many business trips remembering everything except one crucial item such as toothpaste, extra socks or a belt. These omissions added complexity and cost to my travels. Other times, I find I packed five shirts for a two day trip. A little planning prior to leaving will save time and help your road trip be much more enjoyable.

Depending on your mode of transportation, some other items that may be worth packing include caffeinated energy drinks, a GPS, camera with extra batteries, charge cords, a satellite radio, and a travel pillow.

What else do you do, or should do, before leaving on a road trip? You should perform routine maintenance on your vehicle. This will ensure that your road trip does not have any unscheduled stops or mishaps. Routine maintenance includes checking fluids (oil, antifreeze, and transmission), belts and hoses and inflating the tires to the manufacturer's recommended OE pressure. If you are not mechanically inclined, take your vehicle to a mechanic a few weeks prior. The cost should be minimal and is quickly offset when weighed against the prospect of having to deal with sketchy auto repair shops in parts-unknown.

What would you "pack" to prepare for your "Work Road Trip" in a static role? First, you would pack anything that would help you incorporate some variety in your day and make it more enjoyable. It could be making reservations for lunch with your spouse, or packing the book you want to enjoy during break or scheduling time with the employee in another division you want to work with.

If you are a trumpet player moving to the Jazz ensemble, you would pack your plunger, aluminum mute and sheet music. If you are a pilot wanting to explore new places on a new route, you would pack tourist guidebooks, maps and a pair of walking shoes. If you are an assembly line worker moving to another station, you would pack any tools, equipment or safety items that are needed.

And like checking the fluids on your vehicle before departing, how would you prepare your schedule prior to leaving on your road trip? Identify key task, due dates, meetings and events that you must accomplish in your static role. Work ahead as much as possible and free up additional time so you will not be rushed during your trip. Like preparing for a road trip on a motorcycle, the better you prepare ahead of time, the better your "Work Road Trip" will be.

Step #4 – Eat, Sleep, Drink, Move On

Once you have been on your road trip for awhile, you will want to take a break because of stiff muscles, a full bladder or heavy eyelids. Rest Areas, or Travel Plazas, were constructed in the 1940s and 50s as highways expanded cross-country as a place for weary travelers to rest. While there, drivers and passengers find food, rest and relief allowing them to proceed on their road trip refreshed.

Every employee, whether static or not, needs to visit a rest stop while on their "Work Road Trip." This rest stop may be a weeklong vacation to Disney, a lunch break away from the office or reading the newspaper in the break room. By taking time to rest, you will be reinvigorated and able to continue your work day.

It is even more important for static employees to heed this advice. Why? Because non-static employees, one's that progress to positions of more responsibility or just change, constantly face new challenges that make the day go by faster. A static employee may be more prone to burnout or stress because of the repetitive nature of their jobs. When you take a vacation you should not think about work while you are away or it will not be taking a vacation. You will not get the mental rest you need to reinvigorate your desire to do a good job. Sometimes this can be the most difficult thing to do. Cruises are a great way to fix this problem. Because internet and cell services are so limited, passengers are forced to take time out from their work. That fact, along with a few tropical drinks and the lull of the ocean breaking against the bow may make coming back to work difficult to do.

Step #5 – Wheelies, Stoppies and Knee Draggin

As a road trip progresses, the rider will find themselves more comfortable with their environment and may become bored with the trip. Once this happens, most riders want for more interaction to alleviate the boredom and have some fun. Motorcyclists have a few options to challenge them during their ride. These include doing wheelies (popping the front wheel up and riding on the back wheel), stoppies (abrupt stop with the front brake only so that the back wheel comes off the ground) and knee draggin (aggressively going through curves so the rider's knees touch the pavement). Not all exactly legal but exciting none the less.

As an employee, once you are comfortable in your position you may want for more challenge and excitement as well. What activities could be considered "work wheelies?" A work wheelie would be anything that takes your position to the next level of engagement and excitement. Challenge yourself to learn another facet of your company, incorporate your hobby into your business day, or become the expert in your position. Any of these will assist you in becoming a greater asset to your company.

A trumpet player could become the resident expert on the differing tonalities of jazz trumpeters. An airline pilot could become certified on additional types of airplanes and jets. Or an assembly line worker could master different assembly stations. Whatever is done, it will keep the work day fresh and keep the employee challenged, stimulated and satisfied.

Step #6 – Drafting's Not Just for NASCAR and Architects

Drafting is a term used in car racing to describe the practice of one car following another car very closely bumper-to-bumper. This practice diffuses the airflow and allows both cars to go faster than what one car could do by itself. Motorcycles do not draft in the same terms but they do follow each other as a way to enhance their riding experience. While one motorcyclist drafts behind another, they can follow their line of travel and minimize risks. Whether it is a group of sport bikers playing catch the leader through the mountains or cruisers on the highway, drafting behind each other makes everything less stressful and more enjoyable. It is a way that a rider can relax and enjoy the ride.

Static employees can do the same. They can draft behind other employees who are leading the charge against a directive. In the same way two race cars that are drafting together can go faster than one, two employees who are working together can go faster as well. Pair up with another static employee who is doing the same job function as you and compare best practices, work schedules and progress against assigned tasks. As you discuss the challenges you both face daily, some positive synergies will reveal themselves to you. You will probably find simple

ways you could help each other out and save time.

An example would be when a colleague of mine worked on an Account Team. Every four to six weeks, he would perform a price check of Kraft's products in different channels. He did this for only the products for which he was responsible. But he found that his peers were doing the same task at different times. He and his peers decided to combine their efforts and rotate price checking responsibilities among them so that only one was working on the task at a time. This reduced the workload for all and only added minimal time during each visit. The work was still being accomplished but it was being done in a much more productive way that benefitted everyone.

By doing these six steps, by going on a "Work Road Trip," your static position will become more enjoyable and challenging. You will increase your asset value to your company and be seen as "one to keep" if times become tough. Begin your road trip today by planning your route for tomorrow. See you on the blacktop!

Darren MacGillivray arrives back from his training ride. He is tired, sweaty and glad to be home. He found that he needed the preparation he put into his training ride. He rested when his leg cramped, stopped at the grocery store when he ran out of sports drink and used his spare tire tube when the one he was using got cut somewhere along the way. Being prepared helped him complete his ride successfully. Now he plans on preparing for work to ensure that he is just as successful tomorrow.

**For more information on the C Different Foundation, please visit their website at www.cdifferent.org.*

The Toonalution of ...Staying Put

Conclusion

This book does not have all of these answers and it is meant to give a creative, positive spin of the business world. Times are challenging and big business will continue to do more with less. Nothing is guaranteed even when best efforts are put forth. Recognize that fact and own your career path to the best of your abilities. Be the best asset to your company that you can be. No one can ask any more of you. Start your own Toonalution in your company by challenging your coworkers and manager to better themselves by taking a creative and positive approach to your career path.

For more information on Starting Your Own Toonalution,
please visit www.toonalution.com.

Acknowledgements

A special thank you to Jennifer Steffens one of my biggest supporters, initial draft editors and older sister.

Toonalution Outakes of the Auction Winners

John Stanley

Jason Dixon

Tara Parker

Bruce Cox

Veronique Carter

Greg Johns

Tom Darrow

Laura McBrien

Jennifer Steffens

Kathy Stewart

Harriett Frankel

Darren McGillivray

A Toonalootion of...A Scavenger Hunt!

Search the book for the answers to the Scavenger Hunt questions and unscramble the blanks for a secret message! Hints are provided in accompanying pictures and the answers are in reading order.

Cover & Preface

1) What high tech tool is Mona using?

___ ___ ___ ___ ___ ___

2) Who's "Missing" in the group illustration?

___ ___ ___ ___ ___ ___ ___ ___

3) What type of physics did I contemplate in the mountains?

___ ___ - ___ ___

4) In front of what kind of sign did I contemplate writing a book?

___ ___ ___ ___ ___ ___ ___ ___ ___

___ ___ ___ ___ ___ ___

1

5) What plant is in the illustration?

___ ___ ___ ___ ___ ___ ___ ___ ___ ___ ___ ___

Toonalution #1

1) How many beakers and/or test tubes did the Scream fellow break?

___ ___ ___ ___ ___

2) What type of pen did I use on my self-portrait?

___ ___ ___ ___ ___ ___ ___

2

3) What phrase is on Venus' surfboard?

___ ___ ___ ___ ___ ___ ___ ___ ___ ___

3

4) Where did the Scream fellow visit while in New York?

___ ___ ___ ___ ___ ___   ___ ___

___ ___ ___ ___ ___ ___   ___ ___ ___

4

Toonalution #2

1) What position is Jason preparing for?

___ ___ ___ ___ ___ ___ ___   ___ ___ ___ ___ ___

5

2) What instrument is the viola playing? ___ ___ ___ ___ ___

6

3) Venus and Mona charged $ ___ . ___ ___.

4) This "Gamblin' Man" has ___ ___ ___ ___ ___ ___ eyes.

Toonalution #3

1) What is the wiener dog's name? ___ ___ ___ ___ ___

2) The are ___ ___ ___ ___ flowers on this cute five year old.

3) What did Vicky the Vac accidently suck up?

A ___ ___ ___ ___ ___

7

Toonalution #4

1) How much more drive do sales reps now have? ___ ___ %

2) What is Sweettooth eating? ___ ___ ___ ___

8

3) The "Justice Girl" is weighing ___ ___ ___ ___ ___ ___.

Toonalution #5

1) What Shakespearian play is the skeleton paying tribute to?

___ ___ ___ ___ ___ ___

9

2) What highlighted word shows up in the Talent Show sign? ___ ___ ___ ___

3) What song is the unemployed appendix singing? ___ ___ ___ ___ ___

4) What is in Dr. Donut's IV? ___ ___ ___ ___ ___

5) What is Dr. Macintosh's worm eating? An ___ ___ ___ ___ ___

10

Toonalution #6

1) How many eggs are in the clubhouse? ___ ___ ___ ___ ___

2) Who's hiding in Jay's blueprints? ___ ___ ___ ___ ___ ___ ___

11

3) What "may need more work than they appear?"

___ ___ ___ ___ ___ ___ ___

12

4) What is the barricade's name? ___ ___ ___

5) What is the elephant's favorite movie? ___ ___ ___ ___ ___

6) Venus' missing ___ ___ ___ ___ ___ ___ ___ ___ was excavated in this chapter.

7) What TV show does the license plate pay tribute to?

The ___ ___ ___ ___ ___ ___ ___ ___

Toonalution #7

1) The owner of this "pad" has a sleeping neighbor.

The owner is a ___ ___ ___ ___ ___.

13

2) This "referee" has ___ ___ ___ ___ ___ stripes.

3) ¿Cuántas flores son en la guitarra de la hormiga? ___ ___ ___ ___

4) What type of animal is this? ___ ___ ___ ___ ___ ___ ___ ___ ___ ___ ___

14

Toonalution #8

1) This "Little Buddy" is unsinkable. He's an ___ ___ ___.

2) What iconic cartoon character is "caught" by Scream?

___ ___ ___ ___ ___ ___

15

3) Who's holding this chap? ___ ___ ___

16

4) What school took a rafting field trip?

___ ___ ___ ___ ___ ___ ___ ___ ___ ___ ___

17

Toonalution #9

1) The elephant enjoys jumping over ___ ___ ___ ___.

2) Mona is holding a ___ ___ ___ remote.

3) What game are the girl's playing? ___ ___ ___ ___

___ ___ ___ ___ ___ ___

18

4) What video game does Jay love? ___ ___ ___ ___ ___ ___ ___ ___ ___ ___ ___ ___ ___

19

Toonalution #10

1) What's between "Peak" and "Poor?" ___ ___ - ___ ___

2) This Vette is from 19___ ___.

3) Let's Start a ___ ___ ___ ___ ___ ___ ___ ___ ___ ___ ___

20

4) What part does Jay still need to upgrade? ___ ___ ___ ___ ___ ___

21

5) What trophy toon is out of place? ___ ___ ___ ___

22

___ ___ ___ ___ ___ ___ ___ ___ ___ ___

Toonalution #11

1) Which 1970's sitcom character is Jay dressed as? The ___ ___ ___ ___

2) The cartoon version of Superman SHOULD live in

___ ___ ___ ___ ___ ___ ___ ___ ___ ___ ___ ___ ___

23 24

3) This chimp is just plain ___ ___ ___ ___ ___.

25

4) Who's being launched into the wild blue yonder?

___ ___ ___ ___ ___ ___ ___ ___

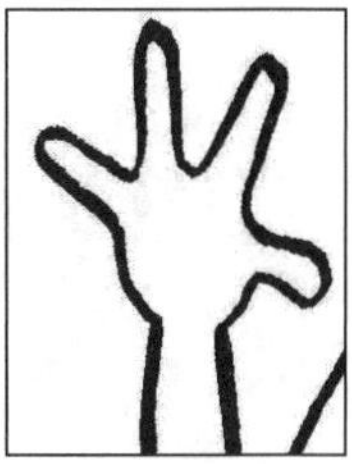

Fill the numbered blanks for a secret message
just for you looney readers that did the Scavenger Hunt!

1 2 3 4 5 6 7 8 9 10 11 12 13

14 15 16 17 18 19 20 21 22 23 24 25

Now unscramble them!

15 6   3 7 5 18   14 25

11 22 19 17 8   16 13 20 23

1 21 2 10 9 24 4 12

For an additional Toonalution of a Scavenger Hunt,
visit our website at www.toonalution.com.

The Toonalution of ...Diversity

The Toonalution of ...Human Resources

The Toonalution of ...Fitting In

Toonalution Puzzle

Collect all puzzle pieces by attending Author signings and receive a **FREE** Toonalution gift.

Hidden Characters Revealed in Final Puzzle Piece!

The Toonalution of ...the Author

Greg does not consider himself a professional writer or illustrator but rather a creative businessman who enjoys leading a team as much as he does drawing a toon. He also enjoys golf and nature....and the two should never meet.

To "Start Your Own Toonalution," or for licensing opportunities, please visit www.toonalution.com.